mara
BOOKS

2840 West Rowena Avenue

a celebration
of laughter

Edited by Werner M. Mendel, M.D.

Library of Congress catalog card number 70–119759

International Standard Book Number 0–87787–000–4

Preface

This is a book of celebration.

We celebrate Martin Grotjahn. We celebrate his sixty-fifth birthday and his creativity. He has lived as a physician, a psychoanalyst, a teacher, a cartoonist, an author and researcher, and as a friend to human existence. In June of 1969, his students, his patients, his friends, and his admirers gathered in Los Angeles to rejoice in Martin Grotjahn's life and his study of laughter.

This book celebrates human laughter. In these essays, historians, satirists, psychoanalysts, psychologists, and psychiatrists follow the trail of laughter from the joke to happiness. They explore the laughter which relieves tension. They admire the razor sharpness of the laughter which expresses hostility. They observe the laughter which covers the hurt. They look at the laughter which is creativity. They envision the new laughter which arises from the world of freedom and leisure, a laughter which promises to pave our road from the world of drivenness and guilt to the world of creative living. The reader who now joins in the celebration brings the responsive understanding necessary for the study of laughter.

Each of us goes this way only once. Each of our existences is a celebration of life. Our laughter is the music of that celebration. Through tens of thousands of years of development and technological advances human beings have retained a sense of humor in their quest for happiness. Laughter is surely a major survival resource.

Most of all, this book celebrates life. It celebrates the life of each human being who has ever laughed.

Werner M. Mendel, M.D.
Department of Psychiatry
University of Southern California
Los Angeles, California

Contents

Contents

a celebration
of laughter

Martin Grotjahn

1/

Interview with Martin Grotjahn

Martin Grotjahn has written more than three hundred scientific essays spanning a wide range of theoretical and practical aspects of psychiatry. His books include *Beyond Laughter, Psychoanalysis and the Family Neurosis, Psychoanalytic Pioneers,* and *The Symbol,* soon to be published by Mara Books.

Dr. Grotjahn studied in Berlin when it was a city of great intellectual ferment. He combined his duties as an assistant at the University Clinic of Berlin with his study of psychoanalysis at the Berlin Institute, supplemented by long debates among the pioneers of psychoanalysis living in Berlin at the time.

Several years after Dr. Grotjahn married Dr. Etelka Grotjahn, they began facing the necessity of leaving Germany, but hoped that the Hitler regime would surely be over in two years. An incident convinced the Grotjahns to leave: One day as Etelka was carrying the baby out of a taxi, some Jews on the sidewalk were assaulted by a mob. At that moment the Grotjahns knew they could not bring up their son Michael in that environment. Unaware of the welcome they would receive in America, the Grotjahns started procedures to come to the United States. By invitation from the Menningers Dr. Grotjahn went to Topeka, Kansas and worked at the Menninger Clinic for two years. (Etelka was worried that

1

if they went back to Europe after their stay in Topeka, they would never have seen America!) He worked for five years as a staff member of the Institute of Psychoanalysis in Chicago. After four years in the American army, the Grotjahns settled in southern California.

The door to Dr. Grotjahn's office in Beverly Hills has only his name, without any title or description of his practice. The waiting room has large books of photographs. Dr. Grotjahn invited me into his work office. The door to the consultation room was open, showing well-used chairs arranged in a circle with footstools, and a soft black couch. Both rooms were lined with neat bookcases. A special set of shelves held paper supplies and Dr. Grotjahn's many reprints. We sat down to talk. Dr. Grotjahn put his feet up and leaned back into his thoughts.

INTERVIEWER: How did it happen that you went into psychiatry and psychoanalysis?

GROTJAHN: When I was a boy of four my father asked me, "What do you want to be when you grow up?" My answer came without doubt, "Irrenarzt" (the old-fashioned German word for psychiatrist). When I ask myself now, sixty years later, "What have I been?" I answer, "A witness to my time." And what did I get out of it? I have lived seven hundred lives, or perhaps a thousand, I have been young and old, man and woman, son and father, happy and not so happy, manic-depressive, and schizophrenic (at least in my dreams). I have been a German and an American and finally I have become a citizen of the world. I have tried to become an existential man in charge of myself and in contact with my unconscious. This has given my life a new dimension. I mostly feel like a mountain guide who has climbed mountains all over the world, alone or with my patients. The mountains, symbolizing the difficulties of human life, are still there, but by now some of us became experts in climbing, while others got lost or gave up.

INTERVIEWER: Was there any question that you would be a physician?

GROTJAHN: I come from a family of physicians, I am the fourth generation and my son is the fifth. There was no question about my choice. My father had told me not to even bother learning any other language besides German. Perhaps that explains my difficulties with English.

INTERVIEWER: Have you had many difficulties with English?

GROTJAHN: Passing through New York and later through Chicago on the way to the Middle West, I was shocked that Americans really spoke English . . . nothing but! I felt like a child who could not understand the language of the adults. They treated me indulgently, like a prematurely matured, gifted child. The change of language is of special importance to an analyst who depends almost completely on verbal communication. I was near despair since listening to people and talking to them was all I had to offer. In my case it led to an elaborate rethinking of my entire analytic orientation. During my first stay in New York, I visited A. A. Brill, friend and translator of Sigmund Freud, who spoke only English for good educational reasons—he never suspected me of not knowing enough English. The four years of work as an army psychiatrist made me feel that I had earned my right to be accepted by this country; the accent remained, to my regret.

INTERVIEWER: How did emigrating affect you?

GROTJAHN: Life after immigration repeats infancy in its helplessness. It repeats the experience of death, rebirth, and adolescence with its identity crises from its uprootedness. To go through all this again as a man is painful, and I would not especially care to repeat it. One change of country is enough of a challenge in my lifetime. Once, it is a strengthening experience, like an initiation rite where the mother's child is symbolically killed and the man is born. The immigration experience contrasts man's basic hope for recognition with his fear of failure. It was as castrating an experience as an adult can have. To be an analyst was not much help since outer reality was all-important and inner reality had to wait. In Berlin I had been the son of a famous father. In the Middle West where I started my struggle with America I was myself. I cannot say that what happened this first year was the emergence of a new identity—but it was a time during which a part of me died and a new person emerged. I remained a kind of curious sightseer. Luckily, I could keep my mind open and could combine the European attitude of the skeptical investigator with the American attitude of always hopefully looking for new and better tools in therapy. I was not really adjusted nor was I maladjusted. I remained unadjusted but happy in my ivory tower with doors and windows open for people to come in and for me to look out.

INTERVIEWER: How did you feel about leaving Germany?

GROTJAHN: Before I could settle into the state of being unsettled, I had to work out a problem which had been activated by my first visit to Germany after the war. I had survived the agony and death of my native country. I had escaped. I felt guilty living in beauty, health, and the undisturbed search for insight. I felt guilty for being alive. I worked hard for psychoanalysis and hoped for recognition and gratitude. But I earned misunderstanding and ingratitude. I discovered that I asked for unnecessary trouble from colleagues, friends, students, fellow-workers, everybody. It dawned on me that what I was doing was like waving a red flag at them so that they would charge at me. I learned my lesson before it was too late and before I had hurt anybody but myself in my need to atone for an unconscious guilt. No one can walk into the future without pain and conflict, which belong to growth and maturation. Now after forty years as a psychiatrist, of living half of my life in Germany and the other half in America, I finally enjoy a quiet happiness in California, "the America of the Americans," where everybody is an immigrant.

INTERVIEWER: How did you get started in your work here in the United States?

GROTJAHN: The alienated man in modern America welcomed the alien from Europe in whom he saw an expert in the art of dealing with problems of existence. This welcome was a great help. I thought I had to show what I could do. It took me some painful experiences to realize that my professional capacity was taken for granted and that my American colleagues were eager to show me that they, too, were analysts. Witnessing the work of Franz Alexander and his team in Chicago developed in me my opinions which ripened later into the widening of my psychoanalytic approach in family therapy, group therapy, and the special aspects of training and treating psychiatrists. I slowly accepted the fact that even in the new world I would have to proceed in personal isolation. Americans saw in me the German and Germans saw in me the American. My Jewish friends never completely forgave me my Prussian background. I always had the impression that they would have respected me more if I would have followed what they thought was my duty: to fight my brothers on the home front as Freud had suggested to non-Jewish analysts in Germany. The Prussians suspected me as a man who left to join the enemy. Psychiatrists thought of me as an analyst and some psychoanalysts classified me as an innovator. I always thought of myself as a clinical observer. I finally had to learn that the truly independent person is loved by no one. The insight helped and when I finally accepted it, it was no longer really true.

INTERVIEWER: If you had a second choice of career, what would it be?

GROTJAHN: As a farmer or a gardener. It is as if I am growing many cabbages and they become cabbages. I have some roses and they become roses, too. And once in a while I watch an orchid bloom. I water my garden four times a week, snip a little here and there, and provide fertilizer. Being a psychiatrist is like being a gardener!

INTERVIEWER: Do you get tired of listening to patients? Don't you hear many of the same stories after all those years behind the couch?

GROTJAHN: No. It gets easier. I am working freer and the understanding becomes more clear. The different aspects of resistance still fascinate me and group interaction becomes more and more the focus of my research.

INTERVIEWER: How long have you been married?

GROTJAHN: After I had been married to Etelka for eight years I discovered that she was a woman and not only a female physician. We lived independent lives in Berlin; she worked at her hospital and I worked at mine. Then one day she said we should have a baby. Our marriage of forty-three years has been a living study of intimacy. My marriage is based on studying one woman and loving her. She is my feminine half. We may have fewer problems than most, for which I give full credit to my wife. Psychoanalysis has spoiled me for social human contact. I go rarely to parties but I like to watch Etelka in relation to other people.

INTERVIEWER: How does your son Michael react to having a successful father?

GROTJAHN: He recently said, "The stories about my father get stranger and stranger—and truer and truer."

INTERVIEWER: What work are you doing now in your research?

GROTJAHN: In recent years, and after my work on *The Symbol*, I became interested in group process. My research in the individual has led naturally to the study of interaction in groups. Sometimes I am the observer, sometimes the participant. And now, it is soon time for my next appointment.

Lori Mendel

2/

Humor in America

Robert Sklar, Ph.D.

Whatever form American humor takes in the future, the comedy of violence, extravagance, and grotesque exaggeration will continue to express fundamental aspects of American culture and society.

When America was young a traveler in the West could never tell what he might find over the next rise in the road or beyond another bend in the river. There might be Davy Crockett himself, astride an alligator or riding the lightning, grinning his fierce, hyena grin that curled the bark off trees; or the Devil-Jack Diamond-Fish, a bullet-proof creature ten feet in length, that Audubon the naturalist, solemn-faced but tongue-in-cheek, described to a visitor from France. One spring day in 1808, walking along the docks at Natchez, a New Yorker, Christian Schultz, Jr., came upon two drunken flatboatmen in an argument. "One said, 'I am a man; I am a horse; I am a team. I can whip any man *in all Kentucky*, by G–d.' The other replied, 'I am an alligator, half man, half horse; can whip any man *on the Mississippi*, by G–d.' The first one again, 'I am a man; have the best horse, best dog, best gun, and the handsomest wife in all Kentucky, by G–d.' The

9

other, 'I am a Mississippi snapping turtle: have bear's claws, alligator's teeth, and the devil's tail; can whip *any man*, by G–d.' This was too much for the first, and at it they went like two bulls . . . " They were fighting, Schultz later learned, over a Choctaw woman. What Schultz encountered that April day along the Mississippi was almost the archetypal expression of humor in America. The battle of the riverboatmen contains nearly all the themes and elements that have gone into the most creative, most enduring forms of American humor—grotesque imagination, extravagant bragging, sexual competition, and the climactic eruption of violence.

From the beginning of the nation there were people who sensed that humor was different in America from humor in the old world, and they always singled out the extravagant and grotesque exaggerations like the Crockett tall tales, Audubon's mythical fauna (he invented others besides the Devil-Jack Diamond-Fish), and the boasting of Mississippi boatmen, whom early newspapers took quite naturally to calling "half-horse, half-alligator creatures." Even the English, who were usually most reluctant to give the culture of America any praise at all, were willing by the 1830s to place the mother country's stamp of approval on a separate American style of humor, a "national American humour," as one English reviewer wrote, expressing "the convictions, customs, and associations" of the nation. Perhaps someone along the way may have considered this a backhanded accolade, and was discomfited by the idea that the grotesque and the extravagant represented the essential convictions, customs, and associations of the United States. But the most stimulating and influential students of humor in America—particularly Constance Rourke in her *American Humor: A Study of the National Character* (1931) and Walter Blair in his *Native American Humor (1800–1900)*, (1937)—have embraced the theory that American humor is an autonomous product of national character and national culture, and this view has strongly shaped the study of humor in America for a generation or more. We need now to subject this perspective on American humor to a thorough reconsideration, not only because our conceptions of character and culture have changed over the decades, but also because we live in a time when every such claim for the special nature of America ought to be held up for scrutiny.

The difficulties in defining a separate and distinct American humor stem, to begin with, from the larger problem of identifying a purely American cultural experience of any sort, except in the gross sense of one which takes place within the United States. Like other assertive, self-proclaimed revolutionary societies, the Americans have made vast claims for cultural originality and inventiveness. But our language, and many of our customs and institutions, derive from the English background of our colonial years, and our peoples have brought with them the cultures and traditions of Europe, Africa, and Asia, as well as absorbing much from the native Indian populations. Moreover, humor is far more universal a human trait than other aspects of culture, and we share many of our favorite jokes and stories with savage societies and monarchical kingdoms. All of these considerations were known to the writers of the 1930s who described a native American humor and a distinctive national character. Perhaps, in retrospect, we should look upon their formulations not as theories but as tropes, as creative metaphors which enabled them to take seriously and examine sympathetically many unexplored and previously deprecated areas of American popular culture. In this manner we may be grateful for their perceptive and enduring insights about culture and humor in America, without belaboring the inadequacies of their concept of national character, whether as psychology or as social history. In the untapped resources of American popular humor they thought they had found a mirror reflecting an undiscovered, unadorned, real American world; they did not realize that they had stepped through the looking glass into an independent realm of humor in America, a world with values and boundaries all its own.

Young America *was* different, to be sure, from other nations. It represented not only the first effort to create a republican form of government over a large territory, but was also the first country in the modern world where an equality of condition among its white citizens seemed so much a living possibility, and even so much a fact—what Alexis de Tocqueville meant when he called his famous study *Democracy in America.* Democracy and equality worked together in a mutually enhancing relationship with the most competitive economic system the modern world had yet seen, and a developing ideology of philosophical and economic individualism. The United States was also the most literate country in the world, an achievement which was founded on the Protestant effort to make every person capable of reading God's Word for himself, but which contributed significantly to the development of equality as a condition and as a goal. And literacy provided the basis for the creation of national newspapers which, considering the dispersed population and the difficulties of travel, played an unusually effective role in the broad dissemination of culture.

The consequences of these unique American political, social, and cultural forms pervaded every aspect of national life, and the emerging American humor, which was attracting international attention in its own right, was bound to reflect them. But in what way? The themes of equality, individualism, and competition are as evident in early American humor as are the themes of exaggeration, boasting, and violence. But who devised such themes, and to what purpose? One basic problem is that we have only a written record to guide us. Some have argued that the fundamental American humor is a folk humor, arising out of the democratic mass, expressing the deepest instincts and values of the lost world of everyday popular life and culture. But that humor comes down to us only by its preservation in the books, magazines, and papers of the time. We need to know about the background and methods of the men and women who wrote and published humor, and performed it on the popular stage; the evidence we have presents the origins and purpose of American humor in an ambiguous light indeed.

For almost all of the American humorists in the formative pre-Civil War years of American humor were members, of the conservative elite. Many were editors of conservative newspapers and reviews; some were conservative lawyers and politicians in the conservative Whig party; others were New England Brahmins or members of the Southern plantation gentry. They did not quarrel fundamentally with the broad democratic developments in American society, the ideologies glorifying individualism or the institutions fostering economic opportunity. But they abhorred the manner in which popular democracy was exercising its ego and its ambitions. They despised the people's President, Andrew Jackson, a man they considered bellicose, unlettered, and dangerously irrational. They opposed the aggressive expansionist spirit that was driving the Indians beyond the forward lines of western settlement and grasping for territories held by Mexico. They deplored the bawdy energies of the uncouth, disorderly, disrespectful democratic rabble. The opinions of these conservative editors, lawyers, and politicians, needless to say, were by definition unpopular. Yet they found a way to express their hostility toward the behavior and opinions of popular democracy in a form that could be widely enjoyed and accepted, through laughter and subtle ridicule. Humor thus developed in the early years of the nineteenth century as a conservative device to deflate the pretensions and expose the follies of democracy in America.

The essential comic device of the early American humorists was the mask, the assumption of the democratic persona in order to ridicule, as it were, from within the camp of the enemy. Had their humor taken the form of a direct, unvarnished assault on the intended target—like the satirical shafts H. L. Mencken directed against the American "booboisie" back in the 1920s—its purpose as an act of political and social aggression would have been apparent to all, and it would have failed in one of its primary aims, that of reaching the people against whom it was directed and reshaping their views and their behavior. A satirical story poking fun at the President might be very funny indeed, but a supporter of the President would likely be incensed by it, and renew his opposition to the President's enemies with redoubled vigor. But a story told by an ostensible friend of the President and apparently sympathizing with him, which yet made the President an object of laughter and ridicule, might succeed in disarming the President's supporter and convincing him that the President was after all a foolish and unworthy leader. The most popular and widely-copied conservative humorists succeeded by putting on the mask of common experience and common speech, posing as country farmers or backwoodsmen, writing in a vernacular dialect which was itself an object of laughter and ridicule to the educated, cultivated readers of humorous papers and books.

Nearly all the famous comic characters of the democratic era were masks created by conservative humorists—Simon Suggs, the invention of Johnson J. Hooper, a Whig newspaper editor in Chambers County, Alabama; Simon Suggs, Jr., the creation of Joseph G. Baldwin, a Whig politician who wrote *The Flush Times of Alabama and Mississippi;* Hosea Bigelow, Birdofredum Sawin, and other comic masks in *The Bigelow Papers* of the Boston Brahmin James Russell Lowell. Even the true-life Davy Crockett began his career as a comic legend in biographies and stories invented by conservative writers to foster a popular western-frontier image for the Whig party, to which Crockett, the Tennessee politician, was persuaded to switch his allegiance. One of the most gentle and amusing comic masks created in the heyday of democratic ideology was Major Jack Downing, a character developed by Seba Smith, a Maine newspaper editor, and later appropriated by other conservative writers. Smith made Downing a confidential adviser to President Jackson, and published letters from the major which perfectly illustrate a successful form of using the comic mask to ridicule from the point of view of the ridiculed. On one occasion the major described a Presidential reception in Philadelphia:

> The President shook hands with all his might an hour or two, till he got so tired he couldn't hardly stand it. I took hold and shook for him once in awhile to help him along, but at last he got so tired he had to lay down on a soft bench covered with cloth and shake as well as he could, and when he couldn't shake he'd nod to 'em as they come along. And at last he got so beat out, he couldn't only wrinkle his forward and wink. Then I kind of stood behind him and reached my arm round under his, and shook for him about a half an hour as tight as I could spring. Then we concluded it was best to adjourn for to-day.

The humorous stories of Southwestern writers, though more difficult to condense briefly here, were often considerably more violent. A. B. Longstreet, a patrician Georgia lawyer and newspaper editor, described in a tale, "Georgia Theatrics," from his book *Geor-*

gia Scenes (1835), how he overheard a fight in a thicket of undergrowth when he was out riding one day:

> "You kin, kin you?"
>
> "Yes, I kin, and am able to do it! Boo-oo-oo! Oh, wake snakes, and walk your chalks! Brimstone and—fire! Don't hold me, Nick Stoval! The fight's made up, and let's go at it—My soul if I don't jump down his throat, and gallop every chitterling out of him before you can say 'quit'!"
>
> "Now, Nick, don't hold him! Jist let the wild-cat come, and I'll tame him. Ned'll see me a fair fight! Won't you, Ned?"
>
> "Oh yes; I'll see you a fair fight, blast my old shoes if I don't!"
>
> "That's sufficient, as Tom Haynes said when he saw the elephant. Now let him come!"

Longstreet dismounted and hurried to the scene of the fight.

> I had overcome about half the space which separated it from me, when I saw the combatants come to the ground, and, after a short struggle, I saw the uppermost one (for I could not see the other) make a heavy plunge with both his thumbs, and at the same instant I heard a cry in the accent of keenest torture, "Enough! My eye's out!" . . . . "Now, blast your corn-shucking soul!" said the victor (a youth about eighteen years old) as he rose from the ground—"come cutt'n' your shines 'bout me agin, next time I come to the court-house, will you? Get your owl eye in agin if you can."
> [Filled with horror and loathing, Longstreet ran after

the youth, calling him to account.] The boy turned back, and said sarcastically, "You needn't kick before you're spurr'd. There a'n't nobody there, nor ha'n't been nother. I was jist seein' how I could 'a' fout." So saying, he bounded to his plough, which stood in the corner of the fence about fifty yards beyond the battle-ground.

"I went to the ground from which he had risen," Longstreet ends the story, "and there were the prints of his two thumbs, plunged up to the balls in the mellow earth, about the distance of a man's eyes apart; and the ground around was broken up as if two stags had been engaged upon it." One smiles with relief as the grotesque and incongruous elements of Longstreet's tale are revealed, yet the horror and the terror of the story remain, as well as Longstreet's social message.

So the grotesque exaggerations and extravagant passions of American humorous writing, which the English thought so new and distinctive as to constitute a separate national American humor, were in fact conceived by conservatives to ridicule and rebuke the cruelty and violence they feared in the popular democracy. What possible connection, then, does a humorous tradition created and carried on by a conservative elite have to do with popular culture and the jokes and stories of the people? The relationship between conservative humorists and the democratic culture was of necessity complex and ambiguous. The humorists did not often invent their stories out of whole cloth. As lawyers and politicians they picked up stories told at courthouses and political gatherings, then embellished them with the particular character of their style and their comic mask. A funny story might begin its life in a local newspaper and reappear in other newspapers around the country with place names changed for local interest, until it reached definitive form in a national sporting and humorous magazine like William T. Porter's renowned *Spirit of the Times*. Then it would trickle back down to the local level, to be retold as if it had just happened last week over in the next village. The widespread literacy of the American people and the effective national communications network made it almost impossible to tell the difference between folk humor and commercial humor.

The professional humorists wrote primarily for their own conservative class, to reinforce their political and social power and confidence in an era when the tendencies of democratic rhetoric and politics threatened to erase all distinctions of birth, character, morals, and learning. An urban, educated class, in any case, would be the principal market for humorous books and periodicals. Yet commercial humor occasionally struck a deep vein of feeling in the people. The Crockett legend, for example, began as a calculated effort to create a favorable frontier image for a conservative Whig politician. The political aim was thwarted when Crockett was defeated for reelection to Congress in 1835. But after Crockett went west to fight and die at the Alamo in 1837, his heroic martyrdom transformed him into a popular hero, and scores of Crockett almanacs glorifying the frontiersman's extravagant feats appeared during the next two decades, establishing him as a perennial folk legend in American popular culture.

It is unlikely that anyone can ever distinguish for certain between those elements of early American humor created in the popular imagination and those developed in the minds of conservative professional humorists; what is significant ultimately is the close and harmonious relationship which paradoxically existed between elite criticism and popular self-image. When the humorists described the grotesque imaginations, extravagant boasting, and explosive violence of the people they meant such behavior to appear ridiculous and socially harmful. Yet to many of the common people bragging, exaggeration, and violence were matters of fundamental pride and self-identity. Several possible psychological explanations may be offered, but one at least is firmly anchored in the realities of American ideology and social structure: The democratic era in American culture produced more than one version of an extreme theoretical individualism, but American society made it very difficult for individuals to express such independent self-reliance in their social, economic, and personal lives. For many lower class Americans the only way they could assert the validity of their theoretical individualism against the reality of severe social constraints was through bragging, tall tales, and violence.

There is one additional strand that ties the ridiculed popular culture to its conservative humorist critics. Whites of all social classes and cultural backgrounds had similar problems of social control and antipathy in relation to black slaves and free Negroes. The device of the comic mask which made it appear as if the ridiculed object were ridiculing himself proved even more effective as a white tactic against blacks than as a conservative tactic against popular democracy, for the whites were the powerful majority, where the conservatives had been only an influential minority. The minstrel show began to appear on the popular stage in the 1820s and within a decade or two the white performer in blackface had become a ubiquitous popular favorite in the American theater, creating an elaborate vernacular dialect and character type that pervaded American popular culture until the civil rights revolution of the 1960s.

Comic aggression is of course a two-way street, and if black slaves were forced to express their hostility to white oppressors in covert, hidden ways, what prevented the popular democracy from retaliating in kind against the conservative humorists who ridiculed them? Surely there were people with comic talent who believed in democratic values and hated the snobbery and gentility of the self-proclaimed elite. Surprisingly, however, there was very little prose or dramatic humor written from a democratic point of view. Perhaps the writers and intellectuals committed to democracy were able to express their hostilities in more concrete political and social form, or the fervor of their beliefs may have made humor too frivolous and indirect a vehicle. The popular stories and jokes of the people were left to the conservative humorists, to alter and reshape as they chose.

There was, however, one major exception to the general domination of humor by the elite. George Washington Harris, an East Tennessee Democrat, small factory manager, and railroad employee, began as a humorist by writing for the conservative *Spirit of the Times,* but in the 1850s he developed a biting, violent antigenteel and antielite vernacular humor that was not welcome in those pages. His later stories, told through the mask of his comic character Sut Lovingood, were published in Southern newspapers and appeared in a book, *Sut Lovingood's Yarns* (1867). Harris was not precisely a voice of the majority, for he belonged to the minority of secessionist Democrats in the part of Tennessee which favored the Union, and some of his angry humor was directed against the mountain hillbillies of East Tennessee as well as against Yankees, politicians, clergymen, teachers, parents, and other figures of authority. What was significant about Harris' humor, as Kenneth Lynn points out in his admirable study, *Mark Twain and Southwestern Humor,* was that the comic mask truly expressed Harris' views. Whereas Longstreet's "Georgia Theatrics" ridicules the violent farm boy, Harris' Sut Lovingood stories direct all their aggression outward. Harris often dropped the controlling adult voice from his stories, and let Sut's clear-eyed youthful vernacular perceptions stand alone. Almost all the Sut Lovingood stories turn on a violent or humiliating act Sut perpetrates, wittingly or unwittingly, on self-important persons, but one may get the flavor of Harris' comic genius from one of his least violent stories, "Rare Ripe Garden Seed." Wat Mastin marries the widow McKildrin's daughter Mary in April, buys some "rare ripe garden seed" from a Yankee peddler, plants his crops, and goes off to Atlanta to work in the railroad yards for a spell. When he returns in late August he finds Mary with a newborn daughter. Slowly he counts the months, stops at four and a half, and cries out angrily that it's only half enough.

> Missis McKildrin shuck her head sorter onsartin like, an' sez she, "Take a drap more sperrits, Watty, my dear pet; dus yu mine buying that ar rar ripe seed, frum the peddler?" Wat nodded his head, an' looked "what ove hit," but didn't say hit.
>
> "This is what cums ove hit, an' four months an' a half am rar ripe time fur babys, adzackly. Tu be sure, hit lacks a day ur two, but Margarit Jane wer allers a pow'ful interprizin gal, an' a yearly rizer." Sez Wat,
>
> "How about the 'taters?"
>
> "Oh, *we* et 'taters es big es goose aigs, afore old Missis Collinze's blossomed."
>
> "How 'bout co'n?"
>
> "Oh, we shaved down roasin years afore hern tassel'd—"
>
> "An' peas?"
>
> "Yes son, we hed gobs an' lots in three weeks. Everything cums in adzackly

half the time that hit takes the ole sort, an' yu *knows,*
my darlin son, yu planted hit waseful. I tho't then
you'd rar ripe everything on the place. Yu planted
often, too, didn't yu luv? fur fear hit wudn't cum
up."

"Ye-ye-s-s he—he did,"
sed Mary a-cryin. Wat studied pow'ful deep a spell,
an' the widder jis' waited. Widders allers wait, an'
allers win.

At the end of the story Wat's
mother-in-law reassures him, "Make yere mind easy, hit never
works on married folks only the fust time."

Harris was an original; though
the social origins and professional careers of humorists
changed over the years, the nature and form of American
humor remained much as the conservative writers had shaped
them. After the Civil War men of considerably lower social
standing than the elite humorists began to dominate American
comic writing. Many of them began as journeymen printers or
journalists, demonstrated a comic flair, and shifted exclusively
to humorous writing. A few became nationally renowned as
platform storytellers. Humorists like Artemus Ward and Petro-
leum V. Nasby and a dozen others like them were immensely
popular in their day, beloved public figures and household
words, yet with the exception of Mark Twain the journalist-
storytellers of post-Civil War America have been almost completely forgotten. One reason for their eclipse lies in the
equivocal nature of their social position as humorists. As
experienced journalists and men of the world they were capable of creating humor by satirizing the sentimental evasions of
late nineteenth-century American middle-class life. But as
men aspiring to higher social status, and as professionals, they
knew that both economic success and social approval could

only come through the genteel middle-class audience of book buyers and arbiters of manners. Their popularity depended on their use of the familiar comic mask of the ridiculous bumpkin or frontiersman, and though they obviously filled the desires of their middle-class audience, their humor lacks the acute social observation and pungent rancor of the earlier conservative humorists. In a perceptive essay, "How to Tell a Story," Mark Twain also suggested that what was really funny about American humor was not the story but the telling of it—the ability of the storyteller to assume the comic mask and vernacular dialect, and tell the story in a completely deadpan manner, as if he really were the bewildered, ridiculous butt of the tale. The platform skills of the late nineteenth-century American humorists have been lost to us forever.

Mark Twain, the greatest of the nineteenth-century American humorists, was acutely aware of the equivocal social position of the humorist and its effect upon his humor. In many of his characteristic tales and episodes there are masks within masks, as when the storyteller (Mark Twain, himself the comic mask of Samuel L. Clemens) meets another storyteller, who tells (or botches) a vernacular tale; in Mark Twain's first important success, "The Celebrated Jumping Frog of Calaveras County," ridicule is directed inward, within the vernacular story, and also outward, against the genteel narrator who, in the old, conservative manner, was supposed to provide the superior framework for understanding the implications of the vernacular tale. The tensions between the vernacular roots of his creativity and the genteel constraints and values of his social aspirations dominated much of Mark Twain's career. He mastered the dilemma only once, in his great novel *The Adventures of Huckleberry Finn,* begun in 1876 but completed only after much travail in 1884.In *Huckleberry Finn* Mark Twain succeeded, for the first time in the history of English and American literature, in writing a work of fiction entirely in the vernacular. The comic mask is brought to life as an autonomous, independent consciousness, and every judgment is made within the style and the language of the work of art. With *Huckleberry Finn* American humor transcended its character as a weapon of social division and class distinction, and encompassed for the first time within its framework a whole society.

The achievement of *Huckleberry Finn* marked the end of an era in American prose humor. The vernacular comic mask was used effectively by several later humorists, notably by Finley Peter Dunne with his Irish character Mr. Dooley, and the arrival of new immigrants added fresh dialects to the repertoire of vernacular prose humorists and popular stage comedians. But by the end of the nineteenth century the vernacular tradition no longer reflected the principal social conflicts and concerns of the predominantly educated, middle-class audience for prose humor. To men and women who lived in an increasingly urbanized, bureaucratized, technological culture the old beliefs that men struggled with each other to create themselves and their society, party against party, class against class, were reshaped by a new sense that man's great antagonists were large impersonal forces: society, the state, the machine, the system. The educated middle-class citizen began to see himself as the underdog, as the slightly ridiculous human figure in a world of hostile forces and indifferent institutions. American prose humor in the twentieth century gave up some of its grotesque and extravagant features and became more witty, subtle, and urbane, as exemplified by humorists like Robert Benchley, Dorothy Parker, James Thurber, and S. J. Perelman. In a way they turned the everyday language and common experiences of the average man into a comic mask, and the aggressive force of their humor seems at times most pointed when it is directed inward, against the hapless struggles of their meek, civilized Casper Milquetoast antiheroes.

At the beginning of the twen-
tieth century, however, the emergence of the motion picture
as a new art and entertainment form created an extraordinary
moment in the history of American humor—a medium of mass
popular entertainment developed in its formative years free
from the constraints of genteel middle-class cultural control
and economic power. During their first twenty years motion
pictures were largely attended by and made for working-class
people, and creators of the movies were outsiders from
middle-class society, vaudeville performers and immigrant
entrepreneurs for whom genteel aspirations were not yet a
living reality. Thus they were free to create what may be the
only authentically popular expression of commercial humor
in American history—a humor embracing and revitalizing,
through new visual forms, the nineteenth-century humor of
grotesque exaggeration, extravagance, and violence, and,
more importantly, directing its aggressions outward against
authority and power, against the cops and the rich.

The silent comedy, of course,
had no place for vernacular dialect, but its visual form created
unique opportunities for the comic mask, and no movie
comedian utilized them more cleverly than Charlie Chaplin,
the great artist of silent comedy as Mark Twain was the great
artist of vernacular humor. It is instructive to know that Chaplin disliked the urbane prose humorists, for some commentators have tried to equate Chaplin's comic mask of the Tramp
with the ineffectual comic figures of twentieth-century prose
humor. But Chaplin's Tramp possesses exactly what the middle
class comic subjects lack: a strong, precise, freely expressed
antipathy to social distinctions and class pretensions, and a
willingness to exploit the grotesque and extravagant comic
elements to gain his ends. Chaplin's Tramp was a brilliant crea-

tion of what may be called the visual vernacular, and nowhere was Chaplin more inventive with the vernacular tradition than in his reversal of the class uses for the mask. In the nineteenth century conservative and genteel humorists assumed the comic mask in order to ridicule the popular character as if from within. In several of Chaplin's greatest movies the Tramp, by accident or design, masquerades as a genteel figure—as a preacher in *The Pilgrim* (1923), as a rich man in *City Lights* (1931). Thus Chaplin ridiculed gentility as if from within.

With the coming of sound most of the silent movie comedians were swept into oblivion; Chaplin alone continued to make silent comedies as an independent producer. The aggressively antigenteel humor of the early movies was extended in visual and verbal form for a time by the Marx Brothers and by Mae West. Both West and the Marxes came to Hollywood from the Broadway theater, and their styles of verbal humor shared many of the urbane and sophisticated qualities of the prose humorists (S. J. Perelman wrote several of the funniest Marx Brothers screenplays). But the motion picture medium broadened and coarsened their humor, turned their comic masks into natural personalities rather than stage personae, and they directed their aggressive humor against the outside world rather than against themselves. W. C. Fields, who was more ambiguously a figure of outward aggression and self-derision, managed to preserve his comic genius even longer. But as the movies extended their appeal into the middle class, becoming the mass cultural arbiter of taste and values that popular fiction had been in the nineteenth century, gentility eroded the class and social hostilities of movie comedy, taming some comics, like the Marx Brothers, and discarding others, like Mae West. The other mass entertainment media created by electronic technology, radio and television, never had the chance to develop outside the watchful care of genteel culture. In the heyday of radio the most popular program year in and year out was "Amos 'n' Andy," a blackface comedy that represented a more sophisticated, urban form of the minstrel show tradition. Television comedians from the start, even such creative comics as Sid Caesar, worked under strict genteel restraints.

After the World War II critics and commentators bemoaned the decline and fall of American humor. The postholocaust, post-Hiroshima generation could not laugh as easily as men and women once had done. The tame sophistication of prose humor and the bland conformity of radio and television comedians seemed to bear out the most dire prognosis for the survival of humor. Predicting the future of cultural forms, however, is a risky task. At the bleakest moment in the history of American humor, vital, creative comic energy began to express itself. The 1960s became one of the great eras for American humor. But cultural structures and moods change very rapidly in modern American society, and no one can say for certain what will happen to American humor in the years to come.

The sources and outlets for the resurgence of humor in the 1960s, however, may provide some clues to the most likely forms and values to be found in a living American humor. The comic revival began outside the professional institutions of humorous production, the newspaper and periodical press and the electronic mass media. The new humorists of the 1960s emerged from the hip bohemia, like Paul Krassner, founder of the underground magazine *The Realist,* and Lenny Bruce, the night club comedian; they were artists experimenting with new forms, like Claes Oldenburg and Andy Warhol; perhaps most significantly and influentially, they were novelists working in a form that was no longer of central importance to genteel middle-class cultural dominance. Many of the serious, memorable novels of the Sixties were comic novels—Joseph Heller's *Catch 22,* Kurt Vonnegut's *Mother Night* and *Cat's Cradle,* Thomas Pynchon's *V.* and *The Crying of Lot 49,* John Barth's *The Sot-Weed Factor,* Norman Mailer's *Why Are We in Vietnam* and more. Their success helped to loosen up the media, and paved the way for a revival of creative humor in the press and on television, in the work of Art Buchwald and Russell Baker and cartoonists like Conrad and Interlandi, in comedians like the Smothers Brothers and Rowan and Martin.

American humor of the 1960s was called "black humor," but as we have seen, American humor was "black humor" from the beginning—a humor of grotesque exaggeration, extravagance, sexuality, and violence. The blackness of American humor was at first an elitist device to ridicule the popular democracy, but the people embraced extravagance, boasting, violence, and the grotesque as genuine expressions of their own true nature. Gentility dominated American humor for much of the past century, and the pervasive sense of man's helplessness against the forces of society and the state seemed for a time to doom American humor to the self-deprecating witticisms of the average middle-class man, the secret dreams of Walter Mitty and the verbal quips of Bob Hope. Yet the deep social divisions and class distinctions of American society had only been hidden, not eliminated, in the first half of the twentieth century, and when they burst forth again in the 1960s they found expression in the humor of the outsider and the tramp. The comic mask of vernacular crudity, created in derision, has been transformed—from Mark Twain through Charlie Chaplin to the "black humorists" of contemporary America—into a proud expression of cultural authenticity and liberation from genteel repression and liberal blandness. Whatever form American humor takes in the future, the comedy of violence, extravagance, and grotesque exaggeration will continue to express fundamental aspects of American culture and society—not a vague and undefinable American character, but the perpetual struggle over cultural control and creative expression, over the form and direction of social change.

Annotated Bibliography

Constance Rourke's classic study, *American Humor: A Study of the National Character* (1931), remains evocative and stimulating. Walter Blair's *Native American Humor (1800–1900)* (1937) is still the most comprehensive study of the subject, and reprints as well a wide selection from the nineteenth-century humorous writers. Kenneth Lynn has published a briefer and more pointed collection of humorous writings, *The Comic Tradition in America* (1958). Lynn's *Mark Twain and Southwestern Humor* (1959) is excellent both for its perspective on the values and techniques of the elite humorists, and in relating Mark Twain to the pre-Civil War humorous tradition. The best study of Mark Twain as an artist is Henry Nash Smith's *Mark Twain: The Development of a Writer* (1962). Norris W. Yates has written a valuable study of the twentieth-century writers of prose humor, *The American Humorist: Conscience of the Twentieth Century* (1964). For silent movie comedy, the best work is Donald W. McCaffrey's *Four Great Comedians* (1968), which covers Charlie Chaplin, Buster Keaton, Harold Lloyd, and Harry Langdon, and also deals with many other aspects of silent comedy. Richard Dorson's *American Folklore* (1959) presents much valuable information on folk humor and folk traditions. A recent, wide-ranging study of American humor is Jesse Bier's *The Rise and Fall of American Humor* (1968).

1. Bier, Jesse: *The Rise and Fall of American Humor.* New York: Holt, Rinehart and Winston, 1968.

2. Blair, Walter: *Native American Humor (1800-1900).* New York: American Book Company, 1937.

3. Dorson, Richard M.: *American Folklore.* Chicago & London: The University of Chicago Press, 1959.

4. Lynn, Kenneth S.: *The Comic Tradition in America.* New York: Doubleday & Company, Inc., 1958.

5. Lynn, Kenneth S.: *Mark Twain and Southwestern Humor.* Atlantic: Little, Brown & Company, 1959. (An Atlantic Monthly Press Book)

6. McCaffrey, Donald W.: *Four Great Comedians.* New York: A. S. Barnes & Company, 1968. London: A. Zwemmer, Limited, 1968.

7. Rourke, Constance: *American Humor: A Study of the National Character.* New York: Harcourt, Brace and Company, 1931. New York: Anchor Books, 1953 (paper).

8. Smith, Henry Nash: *Mark Twain: The Development of a Writer.* Cambridge, Mass.: Harvard University Press, 1962.

9. Yates, Norris W.: *The American Humorist: Conscience of the Twentieth Century.* Ames, Iowa: Iowa State University Press, 1964.

3/

It Isn't Just *Mirv*

Art Buchwald

The worst thing for a humorist is to know anything about humor.

I know he doesn't mean to do it intentionally, but every time Secretary of Defense Melvin Laird opens his mouth, he scares me. In order to get support for the anti-ballistic missile program, Laird has thrown more Soviet missile threats at us than all the former Secretaries of Defense put together.

We're told that if we don't build an ABM system to protect our Minutemen, the Soviets will be able to wipe them out with their MIRV'S, Multiple Re-entry Vehicles, which they have developed as a first-strike weapons capability in answer to our MIRV—a Multiple Independently-guided Re-entry Vehicle. Our MIRV carries clusters of nuclear warheads as compared to the old-fashioned nuclear missiles, which could only be shot off one at a time.

You would think that MIRV would be the ultimate doomsday weapon in our arsenal, but this is not the case. MIRV will open a whole new generation of nuclear hardware and we might as well be prepared for it.

I have a friend at the Pentagon who said, "MIRV is nothing compared to what we've got on the drawing boards. You should see IRVING."

"What is IRVING?"

"IRVING is the Intercontinental Re-entry Vehicle Injector Nuclear Group. It not only has clusters of missiles, but each cluster reproduces a new generation of missiles *while in flight.*"

"My God," I said, "that should certainly give us more than parity with the Soviets."

"It would, except that we know they're working on IVAN."

"What is IVAN?"

"An Independent Vehicle Anti-IRVING Nike, which has clusters of hydrogen warheads set in nitrogen bombs, which can explode within two hundred miles of an IRVING."

"I'm sure we've got an answer to it."

"We have it in BERNIE."

"BERNIE?"

"BERNIE stands for Ballistic Engineered Re-entry Nuclear Evaporator. It has ten thousand rockets which, when ignited by a cluster of IRVINGS, can hit every major capital in the world."

"Good for BERNIE," I said. "I'm sure the Russians wouldn't start anything once they knew we had BERNIE."

"They know it and we know that by 1987 their answer to it will be MISHA. As you know, MISHA stands for Multiple Intercontinental Supersonic Atom-

32

izer. It is fired *down* instead of up and when it hits the earth's core, it explodes and blows up the entire world."

"Then they have the Doomsday Machine?"

"They will have unless we immediately start work on MORTY."

"I know it stands for Multiple something," I said.

"Wrong. It stands for Megaton Oscillating Re-entry Thick Yield. You fire this weapon through a hidden garbage disposal unit and in twenty seconds it produces a mushroom cloud, not only around the earth but over the entire universe."

"Oh," I cried, "if we can only develop MORTY in time."

"Even if we did," my friend said sadly, "we'd still have to go on. You see, while we're talking, the Soviets are doing their preliminary work on SASCHA. Would you like to know about SASCHA?"

"Could it wait until tomorrow?"

4/

Humor and Paradox

Richard Bellman, Ph.D.

It is clear that upon reading any book on humor that discussions of humor are frequently not humorous.

Humor, one of the most intriguing aspects of human consciousness, is an intellectual phenomenon that has been the subject of a great deal of philosophical, psychological, and psychiatric research. Diverse authorities as Bergson (6), Eastman (9), Gregory (10), Grotjahn (11), and Leacock (12), to cite only a few, have analyzed and attempted to explain the various mechanisms behind comedy, humor, and wit.

We wish to discuss here a breed of humor which appears at first sight to be rather esoteric, a type that is intimately connected with paradox, and, indeed, with some fundamental areas of logic. What is noteworthy is that this quite sophisticated brand of humor is becoming increasingly popular and is penetrating more and more deeply into our folk humor.

Our paper is divided into three parts. In the first part we shall explore a number of examples taken from the current scene, particularly the comic strips, which illustrate the humor inherent in a certain kind of paradox; in the second part we shall present a tentative explanation of why we laugh at jokes of this genre; in the third part we shall discuss a classical logical paradox, the "Barber of Seville," and a more formidable cohort due to Russell, which are abstract representations of all the jokes we cite.

There are many ramifications of the topics we discuss, some of which we shall briefly mention.

Let us begin with some simple examples. Bumper stickers containing pithy irreverence are now as common as graffiti. One might say that they are graffiti on wheels, as opposed to graffiti on walls. Capitalizing on this fad are bumper stickers that simply read "Bumper Sticker." Related to these are the signs in many offices that read, "Think" or "Plan Ahead." It is not difficult to explain plausibly why the last two amuse us. The first, however, appears to have a deeper basis.

Let us give two examples from the cinema. In *Breakfast at Tiffany's* Holly Golightly has a cat named "Cat"; in *Bizarre, Bizarre* there is a fervent vegetarian who goes about butchering butchers to express his disapproval of their activities.

Finally, let us note the amusement we feel when we see a tow truck towing a tow truck, or read that a fire station has burned to the ground.

Basically we see that an interaction between the content of the message and the form in which the message is couched stimulates us in some fashion. There is a "feedback" effect which we will examine below.

Let me now cite some examples taken from syndicated comic strips:

Peanuts, February 10, 1968, *Los Angeles Times*
Lucy: You're a very boring person, Charlie Brown.
Lucy: (Yawn)
Lucy: Excuse me.
Lucy: I get bored just talking about how boring you are.

Andy Capp, February 26, 1969, *Los Angeles Times*
Wife: What's going to become of the younger generation, I
       often wonder?
Andy: Oh, they'll probably grow up and wonder what's goin'
       t' become of the younger generation.
Wife: We are sharp this mornin', aren't we?—mind you don't
       cut yerself.

Andy Capp, March 23, 1969, *Los Angeles Times*
Wife: Okay, Kid—Don't drink it dry, leave a drop for
       somebody else.
Andy: If I've told yer once, I've told yer a million times—don't
       exaggerate.
Wife: Heh! Heh! Heh!
Andy: I said something funny?

Peanuts, November 9, 1968, *Los Angeles Times*
Linus: You look kind of depressed, Charlie Brown.
Charlie: I worry about school a lot.
Charlie: I also worry about my worrying so much about
          school.
Charlie: My anxieties have anxieties.

Blondie, May 5, 1967, *Los Angeles Herald Examiner*
Dagwood: I can't get to sleep.

Blondie: That means you must be terribly worried about
　　　something.
Dagwood: I am.
Blondie: What is it?
Dagwood: I'm worried about getting to sleep.

Grin and Bear It, July 4, 1969, *Los Angeles Times*
He: I'll tell you what you did on the old-fashioned 4th of July.
　　You sat around asking whatever happened to the old-
　　fashioned 4th of July.

The question which we wish to
explore is that of isolating the humorous aspects of these pan-
els.

That there is a systematic way
of producing laughter using certain simple general techniques
of the foregoing nature has been known for a long time. St.
Augustine when asked what the Creator was doing before he
constructed the universe responded, "Creating a hell for
people who ask questions like that."

There is the ancient story about
the philospher who was asked why philosophers ask so many
questions. "Why shouldn't philosphers ask so many
questions?" he responded. This is also the standard stall of the
teacher and psychiatrist, "Why do you ask that question?" The
comedian who sees a joke falling flat comments about the failure of the joke, and so on.

The *New Statesman* competi-
tion # 1863, due to Peter Rowlett, reads: Competitors are
invited to compose a short portrait of a typical Weekend
Competition entrant. Bored and wary English instructors familiar with freshman humor assign students to "write themes on
anything—but how to write themes."

Let us cite also the story of the mother who proudly boasts that when her son goes to the psychiatrist all he talks about is his mother. Groucho Marx is reputed to have said that he would not join any club that would accept him as a member.

Finally there is the story that physicists and engineers love to tell which expresses their attitudes towards mathematicians. It seems that they identify with the man who, walking down the street with a bag full of dirty clothes, was looking desperately for a laundry. After walking several blocks he finally spots a store with the sign "Laundry." He rushes in, dumps the bag down on the counter, and asks for the quickest service possible. The man behind the counter looks at him in amazement and says, "We don't clean clothes here." "But, what about the sign on the front of the store?" "Oh," says the man behind the counter, "we only make the signs."

Why then do we laugh at the foregoing?

Let us begin with the observation that incongruity is certainly one basic ingredient of humor. In place of "incongruity," let us use the term "illogic."

We postulate next that a need for order is instinctive in human beings. (For those who don't like the term "instinct," we can exacerbate the situation by making the further statement that all basic reasoning can be postulated to be instinctive. (1) (2)) We can make the existence of this instinct plausible on the grounds that the animal that can discern regularity, and hence irregularity, can predict, anticipate, and thus survive. Logical thinking can be considered then as one expression of this desire for order. The ability to reason provides some control over the uncertainties of a menacing universe.

Consequently, when an event assaults our logic and contradicts our preconception of the natural order of things, a basic instinct is affected. This threat to our well-being produces tension; a mild threat and a mild tension may be relieved by laughter. Laughter disengages us, and has the further value of reassuring us. It helps us feel that the threat is ephemeral and need not be taken seriously. (This is related to the technique of whistling in the dark to dissipate fear.)

With or without acceptance of the postulated mechanism, we know that violation of logic often produces humor. This is a familiar fact. Numerous jokes based on this principle can be cited, as well as many based on too rigid adherence to logic, the Gracie Allen type of humor. Let us note in passing that this rigidity is the principal difficulty in dealing with computers, since neither level nor relationship is perceived by a computer. As completely logical devices, they possess no "common sense," no sense of proportion or balance, nor of their outgrowth, humor. As a matter of fact, it was in attempting to learn how to communicate with computers that interest in these questions was aroused (13).

Assuming the postulated mechanism, the next step is to determine what threat to logic is posed by jokes of the foregoing type. Do we scent some danger to the precarious order we have superimposed upon a chaotic world? It turns out that our instincts are very sound. The paradox that underlies all of the material quoted above is deep-rooted and troublesome. Indeed, it is hopeless but not serious.

It is clear upon reading any book on humor that discussions of humor are frequently not humorous. On the contrary, even the most serious study of pornography is frequently found to be pornographic. The study of logic need not be logical, a fact that seems very surprising only to nonmathematicians. By this statement we mean not only that the discovery of new facts and theories does not proceed in a logical way, but that logic itself contains numerous paradoxes or, more precisely, antimonies. What is amusing is that these antimonies are very similar in form to the foregoing sentences.

The most famous of these paradoxes is that pertaining to the Barber of Seville, a paradox easily stated. At one time, it seems, the city possessed only one barber who was required by law to shave those people, and only those people, who could not shave themselves. The question inevitably arises: Who shaved the barber?

There are a number of ways of extricating ourselves from the cul-de-sac. Perhaps the easiest is to state categorically that it is a contrived paradox. Since we do not accept as reasonable the fundamental premises, the apparent contradiction does not unduly disturb us. We don't feel responsible for the consequences of an artificial situation. We experience the same disdain for the contrived joke, one perhaps that begins: A crocodile and an elephant were discussing their mothers-in-law one day . . .

Fortunately for the gaiety of nations, or should we say notions, the example is bad—but the difficulty is real.

Far more disturbing, and actually profoundly upsetting is the observation that classical mathematical reasoning can lead to paradoxes. One of the finest examples of this is due Russell, centering about the "class of all classes."

For the purposes of discussion let us state that by a "class" we mean a set of objects sharing some specified property, e.g. the class of all psychoanalysts, the class of all patients, the class of all nonobscene four-letter worlds, the class of all concepts.

In the first three of these examples, the class itself is not an object of the same kind as its members. It is neither a psychoanalyst, a patient, nor a four-letter word. But a class is a concept. Hence, the class of all concepts is an example of a class that belongs to itself.

We next divide all classes into two disjoint categories, those that belong to themselves, and those that don't. Question: Does this class belong to itself or not?

It is easy to see that either decision leads to a contradiction. Note, incidentally, that the classical schoolboy "paradox" is an example of this type of reasoning:

1. All generalizations are false.
2. This is a generalization.
3. Therefore, according to the original statement, this last statement must be false.
4. Therefore, there is one generalization at least which must be true.

We see the "feedback effect" working in full force.

Conventional mathematical, logical processes have led to a paradox, a self-contradiction. Our intuition then was not misled—tigers dwell within. What do we do about it? There are systematic procedures for wriggling out of this quandary.

The first procedure examines the nature of the statements and modifies them in such a way as to exorcise the paradox. The basic point is that apparently grammatical, meaningful statements need have no logical content. At first sight this appears quite repellent, an eminently unsatisfying constraint. But recall that one of the prices of a consistent arithmetic is an injunction against dividing by zero. The "grammatical" expression $\frac{1}{0}$ is outlawed. Freedom is not license.

A point we wish to emphasize is the ease with which such "paradoxes," or at least ambiguities, can enter into ordinary speech. it is not at all easy to say precisely what one means, nor, conversely, to point out what is wrong in an argument by someone else leading to an obviously incorrect conclusion. (See the expository article by Tarski (13), and for a new mathematical approach to the study of ambiguous situations, see Zadeh (4), where the concept of "fuzziness" is introduced in a precise fashion.)

Let us digress a moment. Suppose we consider those genes which carry "instructions" for the growth of an organism. Among these are some genes which carry instructions for the construction of the remaining genes. We can postulate that a mutation is the result of some alteration in these instructions, due, for example, to radiation.

This is a plausible and satisfying theory of the development of the vast number of different organisms observed, of the origin of species. Unfortunately, simple calculations seem to indicate that granted the small probability of genetic damage and the high probability of lack of survival of the mutant, enough time has not transpired since the creation of the earth to account for the diversification of species.

If, however, we consider mutation not only in the genetic instructions, but in the instructions for the instructions, then the situation seems more favorable for the theory of evolution. It is intuitively clear that we can have more variation in less time (14).

In our quest for some understanding of the complex and unexpected phenomenon of consciousness, we engage in thinking about thinking. Since there are many ways of doing this, we are forced to engage in thinking about thinking, and so on, an infinite regression. How much then can we understand about our own thought processes? How well can the part understand the whole? Human behavior seems to be more of a task of partial control based upon partial understanding than complete control based upon complete understanding (10).

This brings to mind the jingle of de Morgan (7), "Big fleas have little fleas upon their backs to bite 'em. Little fleas have lesser fleas and so on ad infinitum."

It is a joke of the highest order that logical theories should contain so much that is illogical, and it is a joke of just the right type. As has been noted before, the world was not made for consciousness. It would seem in the face of paradox and puzzle, mischief and mystery, that only a sense of humor allows us to preserve our sanity and that too rigid an insistence on logic must be a symptom of, or produce, insanity.

Bibliography

1. Bellman, R.: Mathematical models of the mind. *Math. Biosci.*, Vol. 1, 1967, pp. 287–304.

2. ———: Adaptive processes and intelligent machines. *Fifth Berkeley Symposium on Mathematical Statistics and Probability*, Vol. IV. Berkeley: University of California Press, 1966, pp. 11–14.

3. ———: On heuristic problem-solving by Newell and Simon. *Op. Res.*, Vol. 6, No. 3, 1958.

4. ———: Kalaba, R., and Zadeh, L.: Abstraction and pattern classification. *J. Math. Anal. Appl.*, Vol. 13, 1966, pp. 1–7.

5. ———: *Adaptive Control Processes: A Guided Tour.* Princeton: Princeton University Press, 1961.

6. Bergson, H.: *Laughter; An Essay on the Meaning of the Comic.* London: Macmillan Co., 1911.

7. De Morgan, A.: *A Budget of Paradoxes,* 2nd Ed. Chicago: Open Court, 1915.

8. Eastman, M.: *The Sense of Humor.* New York: Charles Scribner's Sons, 1922.

9. Freud, S.: *Wit and Its Relation to the Unconscious.* New York: Moffat, Yard and Co., 1917.

10. Gregory, J.: *The Nature of Laughter.* London: K. Paul, Trench, Trubner & Co., 1924.

11. Grotjahn, M.: *Beyond Laughter.* New York: McGraw-Hill, 1957.

12. Leacock, S.: *Humor, Its Theory and Technique with Examples and Samples;* a Book of Discovery. New York: Dodd Mead and Co., 1935.

13. Tarski, A.: Truth and proof. *Scien. Amer.,* Vol. 220, 1969, pp. 63–77.

14. Ulam, S.: How to formulate mathematically problems of rate of evolution. Wistar Institute Symposium Monograph No. 5, *Mathematical Challenges to the Neo-Darwinian Interpretations of Evolution.* Philadelphia: Wistar Institute Press, 1967, pp. 21–34.

5/

The Third Eye of the Cartoonist

Michael Grotjahn, M.D.

The psychoanalyst is a scientist with an amazing array of information and clinical observation delicately interwoven into a theoretical understanding. He must also be an artist who applies his third ear to the music played by the patient. Timing, point and counterpoint must be used creatively. So, also, in humor the listener must be free to allow himself to communicate with a more primary process without fear.

In a similar fashion the viewer of the cartoon is invited to make freer communication with his "third eye." Through this projection onto an inner screen, symbolic representation of psychic life can be viewed anew. Failure to trust this experience is to deny oneself something rich and rewarding.

For years my father has shared with family and friends his psychic life through cartooning. These are his projected treasures of observation. They reveal him not only as an observer and participant in life, but also as a warm refiner of the essence of the spirit of living.

Flowers must be smelled—not only seen.

I didn't know that Narcissus flowers look like me.

They think I am a Flower!

Here I could wait for you by the hour—

Where is everybody?

Oedipus! Your mother wants you!

Only son of Jewish Mother in a double bind.

"I am an experienced mother."
"And I am an experienced child."

In my next life I'll be a Flamingo

6/

The Smile

Edward Stainbrook, Ph.D., M.D.

*Martin Grotjahn's insights
into the enjoyment of laughter have been a joyful
discovery for all of us interested in ourselves and in
man.*

No one is born smiling. The smile genetically hidden in the newborn baby very quickly matures into a potential message formed by the muscular action of the expressive face. It is a facial sign more intrinsic than the psychological unconscious and is evolved out of our behavioral past. The initial responses of the answering older other to the infant's smile are informed by learned meaning and experience. But they may also be considered as biologically given transactions of the releaser evoking the released. The baby's cry brings the mother to cling to; his smile evokes the reassuring countersmile and tender playfulness.

The smile matures and develops vocally into laughter. Then, during the socialization of the person, laughter learns to be joking, sardonic, gleeful, cruel, joyful, self-depreciatory, inhibited, painful, cynical, nasty, seductive, disarming, disclaiming, provocative, explosively tension-dissipating and a myriad other expressive and communicative acts.

The smile has a limited repertory of meaning but laughter is linguistically informed. It enjoys the versatility of language. Sometimes the smile is unvocalized laughter just as sometimes laughter may have no smiling in it.

Hence, the content, the structure, the intensity of the energy-transformation and even the social situation of occurrence are seen to be the result either of coping strategies or of defensive protections engendered in oneself alone or in collusion with others to manage the threatened awareness of anxiety-producing conscious and unconscious needs, fantasies, or memories.

What psychoanalysis has underemphasized is the sociology and culturology of smiling, laughing, and humor. Smiling and laughing are not only expressive of personal psychodynamics, but are also paraverbal communication. They signal appeasement behavior, give and ask approval and liking. They structure dominance and submission; they cue the character of interpersonal transactions as playful, make-believe or metaphorical.

As with the explanations for any human action, the question is not what behavior is conscious and what unconscious. Every act of behavior is shaped by both conscious and unconscious information if for no other reason than that almost all acts of behavior have a history. The task is to decide for any specific action what are the relevant determining variables.

Dr. Grotjahn emphasizes the joyful freedom of being open to oneself. This psychological liberty in being a person allowed him to scan sensitively and broadly the culture of man and to provide new ways for thinking men to transform symbolically their living into helpful meaning. He writes in *Beyond Laughter*, "We need such anxiety-free communication with our unconscious to keep our imagination and intuition alive; to create fully; to form our life. With such rebirth, experienced without guilt, fear or anxiety, performed with grace and with ease, with a smile and with laughter, we become essentially—and incurably—human." (1)

Bibliography

1. Grotjahn, Martin: *Beyond Laughter*. New York: McGraw-Hill, 1957.

7/

Laughter in Psychotherapy

Martin Grotjahn, M.D.

> *Therapy is not a laughing matter, nor is it a weeping wall.*

Laughter is a human response. All recent studies of the psychotherapeutic process show that the response of the therapist to his patients is probably of central importance. While we don't cry with our patients, and while we do not rage with them—or at them—we do feel free to laugh with them.

Sometimes therapists have to dramatize a situation when the patient represses his emotions so deeply that they cannot be reached otherwise. By showing our reaction to the patient's situations we give an example of emotional freedom, and laughter is a sign of freedom. We show that we have emotions, and that we are not afraid of them. We can enjoy them without the fear of losing control. Our emotions should be sincere: Therapeutic skill is not expressed by pretending, but in the ability to judge how much, when, and in what way to show them. Our goal is not impulsiveness but spontaneity; laughter is a model example to express just that. When we laugh "we let the cat out of the bag." We do not need to show our patients we are human but we want at times to give an example of spontaneity, of responsiveness, and the kind of emotional freedom which is part of maturity. In such situations smiling is not enough. A smile is too often a sign of superiority; the therapist smiles only at himself, not at his patients.

Jokes can be used as an excellent method to give an interpretation. The therapist can use it consciously; the patient occasionally does it unconsciously. One patient in group psychotherapy complained bitterly and consistently about repeated, vicious fights between her and her husband. No matter what the group said, suggested, interpreted, or advised, nothing helped. Everything was rejected and the bitter fighting went on. Finally the group therapist said, "Do you know that on Noah's Ark sexual intercourse was forbidden while on board? When the couples filed out of the Ark after the Flood, Noah watched them leave. Finally the tomcat and the she-cat left, followed by a number of very young kittens. Noah raised his eyebrows questioningly, and the tomcat said to him, 'You thought we were fighting?'" After that the group did not wish to hear about the fights any more, implying "If that is the way you want to live, and love, then do so and don't complain."

Interpretations in the form of a joke often bypass the resistance and are acceptable. They have the further advantage that they leave it to the patient to understand the message.

A patient may consider a joke as extraordinarily funny and the analysis of his exaggerated amusement may give the clue to what he does not dare to say directly. A patient of mine was working very well in his analysis and at the end of the hour I summarized my interpretation. He was duly impressed and went on his long weekend seemingly appreciative. The next week he was shaking with laughter when he came to his hour and had to tell a joke he had heard on the weekend, "Three men were going on a fishing trip. It was agreed that one of them was to work as a cook until somebody complained and then the complainer should take his turn. Naturally, there were no complaints. One morning one of the men couldn't stand it any more and turned to the cook and said, 'This really tastes like horseshit—but good!'" The patient could not have symbolized better the conflict between his appreciation for the insight gained and his intention to reject it all as inedible.

Laughter has many meanings. It can be cruel and cynical, and it can be sadistic and bitter. It can be kind and loving, or undisguised hostility. It can be the laughter of triumph or irreverence. The laughter in the psychotherapeutic situation should be the laughter of spontaneity, mastery, and strength and freedom. How a comical situation may show mastery was once experienced by me in the following scene: I had a patient who tried to fight her good appetite by chewing gum constantly. I told her that no one chews gum in my office, so she always disposed of her gum in the waiting room. Once she placed it on the chair and the next patient sat on it. She was filled with digust, near to tears, traumatized. She felt so insulted that the whole trauma of toilet training erupted, was reexperienced and could be analyzed during this hour.

A man with great sensitive awareness for a comic situation and an outspoken sense of humor, and with the gift to dramatize a situation found himself the victim of this predicament. He noticed that something was wrong when he got up from the waiting room chair and felt a slight tug. Immediately he went into an act of performing disgust and embarrassment and shame with grotesque expressions, trying to hide the disaster and to exhibit it accusingly at the same time. He exaggerated more when he saw me helpless in laughter. He gave an example of artistic mastery of an embarrassing and highly annoying situation through a comic performance.

Artistic mastery is not limited to a verbal form or a comic performance. It can also be done in visual forms as in cartoons. A patient wanted to go swimming and felt embarrassed about his obesity and short size compared with the beach beauties on display. So he resignedly drew himself excessively small and ugly, turning to one of the athletes saying "I too was designed to be 6'4"." He then felt that he had mastered a trauma by talking about his obesity.

Existential despair was never better described to me by a patient than when he told the following joke which actually is a tragic short story, "A deep sea diver had descended to the bottom of the ocean and while he was working there he heard through his earphone the voice of his captain, 'Come up quickly—we are sinking!' "

As with all communication telling a joke must be seen as a clue or as a part of the associative communication between the patient and the therapist. All previous examples illustrate this. There is one form of laughter which is difficult for me to understand and which I criticize when it happens in a seminar, in a group, or in individual therapy, and that is the superior laughter at the demasking which is a function of our profession. This form of laughter is found when people begin to understand the dynamics of the unconscious. It sounds to me like the joy of having caught somebody unaware. It was this kind of laughter in the early psychoanalytic Wednesday evenings in Sigmund Freud's house, which were studied by Freud and Theodor Reik, that gave the first insight into the dynamics of laughter.

Laughter is based on a sudden release of hostility in a well-disguised form. The symbolic disguise, however, must not be so complete that it could not be understood by the unconscious of the one who listened. As a rule, the aggression is directed at a third person, an outsider. The joke is between the one who tells it and the one who listens and who gives his approval by laughter.

These dynamics show that laughter in individual therapy can bind the therapist and patient, while in a group it may divide. The one who is the butt of the disguised aggression may temporarily lose his status in the group. This is not always so, because the group also can say, "We are friends—they are our enemies—we are strong together and we laugh at the outsider." If, however, the group laughs at one of its members, a split takes place between "we the group" and "you the target" of our disguised aggression.

In both individual and group situations laughter has to be watched so that it is not used in the service of resistance. This danger is greatest in the group which is ready to switch from hard work to enjoyable entertainment.

In the analysis of a comedian it is necessary on occasion for the therapist to say, "You are not here to entertain me—or yourself. You are here to work. You can amuse me and I don't want to deny it. You have a certain power over me in this respect. I don't want to build up a resistance against your laughter but I also want you to know it can hinder our further progress."

In individual therapy the joke is reenacted between therapist and patient while in the group situation the therapist may remain a witness. This is one of the great differences between individual and group psychotherapy. Here is an example: A man turned to a woman in a group who annoyed him by her heavy smoking, and said, "You really ought to stop smoking." The woman answered, "Young man, I will be seventy next month, so what does it matter?" The young man had the last word, "If you would stop smoking you would be eighty by now."

Some examples may illustrate that group laughter follows the dynamics of individual laughter. One member was in competition with another member and said half jokingly, "After all there is only one Jesus Christ." The other one, with mock sincerity claimed, "Yes, that is quite right and we better leave it that way." According to the situation it was quite clear that he claimed for himself the right to Christian identification.

Once a member of a group came twenty minutes late and another member turned caustically to him and said, "I hear you had a motorboat accident while you took your morning walk," implying that he walks on the water.

Another time one member of a group wanted to give the interpretation that he considered another member of the group hypersexual. He said to him, "I always have been worried about the population explosion but now I am worried about your copulation explosion."

Therapy is not a laughing matter nor is it a weeping wall. Laughter in therapy is welcome like any sign of spontaneity, strength, mastery, and freedom.

8/

The Destructive Potential of Humor in Psychotherapy

Lawrence S. Kubie, M.D., D.Sc.

I welcome this opportunity to congratulate my friend, Martin Grotjahn, on reaching the ripeness of maturity at so young an age. I hope that he will continue to be productive and to grow through a second sixty-five years: because the second sixty-five are always the best.

The late John M. T. Finney, Professor of Surgery at the Johns Hopkins School of Medicine, would often say to his classes: "There is only one 'never' in medicine; never say 'never.'" Then he would sometimes pause reflectively for a moment and add, "No, that is not quite right. There are two. The other is never say 'always.'" With this precept in mind I want it clearly understood that this paper is not designed to persuade anyone *never* to use humor, or that humor is *always* destructive. Its purpose is to make it clear that humor has a high potential destructiveness, that it is a dangerous weapon and that the mere fact that it amuses and entertains the therapist and gives him a pleasant feeling is no evidence that it is a valuable experience for the patient, or that it exerts on the patient an influence toward change.

The interactions between patient and therapist have been studied most intensively in relation to the treatment of one individual at a time. Therefore at this time I will limit my discussion to the influence of humor on the exploratory and therapeutic aspects of individual psychotherapy. This one-to-one model will serve as a point of departure and of comparison for later consideration of the influence of humor on group therapy and in the therapy of childhood. Important though they are, I will not attempt to deal with these problems in this contribution.

As we consider the uses and abuses of humor in psychotherapy we naturally carry over into our thinking some of our experiences with and observations about humor in ordinary social situations. We know that in spite of all that can justly be said about the role of secret malice *(Schadenfreude)* in the social scene, humor can also exert a humanizing influence. It can sometimes be a social lubricant, easing certain kinds of tension and shyness, thus facilitating for *some* participants the opening gambits of conversation and communication. Yet others are sealed off and frightened into silence even by a general atmosphere of joviality, which has no specific reference to anyone present. Sometimes humor expresses true warmth and affection. At other times it is used to mask hostility behind a facade of camaraderie, or to blunt the sharpness of disagreement. And since both can occur simultaneously, it is not always easy to be sure which is dominant. Thus, even in social situations, humor is not always kindly. (1)

If now we examine more closely what goes on in the therapeutic situation, we will find that only under special circumstances does humor facilitate the flow of free associations in a fashion which will further the processes of therapeutic exploration. Too often the patient's flow of feeling and thought are diverted from their spontaneous channels by the therapist's humor, or may even be arrested and blocked. Clearly the patient may pay a high price for our use of this device. Usually the patient realizes how easy it is to use humor as a mask for hostility. He feels the hurtfulness of the true word spoken in jest. Any belated effort to soften such gibes by using some equivalent of the colloquial phrase, "I was just kidding" means nothing to the patient, except that the therapist is "kidding" himself, and especially that he is kidding himself that he was not being nasty.

When the therapist uses humor the patient has the confusing option of wondering whether underneath the humor the therapist is really serious about what he is saying or whether he is "only joking." One may bribe the patient into pretending to accept the humor, but this does not release either his affective responses or his "free associations." In fact when an interpretation is couched in humorous terms as it is presented to the patient, the humor tends in general to constrict the range of the patient's responses, because for the patient to undertake to treat the therapist's humor seriously by associating to it freely is tantamount to correcting the therapist by taking seriously that which the therapist has taken lightly.

Humor may offer a defense against our own anxieties as therapists or against the patient's, either of which may be hard to tolerate. Indeed it may be used as a defense against all forms of psychological pain. The sad "gay" society of the homosexual is an example of this defensive use of humor. Of special importance is the fact that patients frequently use "humor" as a defense against taking their own illnesses seriously. They may mock even their own symptoms in their efforts to evade the acceptance of help. If the therapist steps into this trap by echoing the patient's humor about his symptoms or his ailment, he will reinforce the patient's neurotic defenses.

Many additional considerations make me hesitate to use humor in therapy. I will cite a few of the drawbacks which to me seem important. When in some measure the humor is at the patient's expense he usually feels constrained to join in, if only to prove to the therapist that he too has a "sense of humor." A later study of that patient, especially when made by another therapist, will often show that under the forced smile of his responses to the humor of the prior therapist he had boiled with hidden and persisting anger, the expression of which the therapist's mask of "humor" has made impossible. In fact the therapist's humor tends to make it impossible for the patient to express *any* resentful components in his feelings. Such a bottling up of anger has a destructive effect on any form of psychotherapy; when this impasse is deliberately created not by the patient's neurosis but by ours, it is indefensible.

Moreover, as a similar expression of their neuroses patients often undervalue their own best traits and capabilities, by treating them with mocking humor. To join the patient in such "humor" at his own expense is another way of stepping into a trap set by the patient's neurosis. The result will be to deepen his depression and to stir up an intense but usually well-masked hostility.

This applies equally to many forms of "humor" which are not always intentional. For example, any imitation of a patient by his therapist feels to the patient like mockery, no matter how compassionate and educational the intent may be. On the other hand when we make it possible for a patient to study his own visual and auditory image we avoid any hint of mockery. This is one of the many advantages of the use of what Cornelison has called the "Self-Image Experience." (2) This concern about any deliberate imitation of a patient applies even to responding to a patient's silence by silence. This may drive the patient as deeply into silence as does open mockery or sarcasm or irony. Yet this response to silence has usually been overlooked by those who adhere too strictly to the analyst's preference to make the patient speak up first. This is one of the reasons why, when it is not used with discerning discrimination, the echolalia technique of Carl Rogers is not always evocative.

In general, age differences influence the effects of humor both in social and therapeutic situations. There are differences in the impact of humor between man and man, man and woman, woman to man, or woman to woman. Many special considerations arise about the use of humor in the psychotherapy of children. Among these, of primary importance is the question of the extent to which the patient had been exposed to teasing and mockery in earlier childhood. (These influence the later effects of humor on the therapy of the adult as well.) Consequently the therapist must always remember that he is rarely the first person who has found something "amusing" in the patient's life, in his idiosyncratic patterns of speech and behavior, or in his symptoms. All of these confront us with complicated problems which have far-reaching importance and should be explored separately. In none of these does the patient find much to smile about, although someone other than the therapist has usually smiled or commented mockingly long before. Therefore the therapist will usually inherit a patient's buried reactions to earlier humor. Only at the end of long analytic study will the therapist discover that some of the most destructive people in the story of a patient's life may have been those who always found something to smile about whenever the patient was in pain. This predecessor may have been a father or mother or an older or younger brother or sister, or it may have been a friend or even some relative of a friend or a teacher. The possibilities are almost infinite.

Consider, for instance, a woman patient who was the last in a line of several children, all but the oldest of whom were boys. At first she had been a gay and aggressive little tomboy, accepted as such by her older brothers and their friends with praise, pleasure, and indulgence. Inevitably, the time came when these older brothers and their friends moved into their adolescence, whereupon they wanted not the little tomboy anymore but a little girl with frills, the very kind of girl which they had previously looked upon as "sissy." From that point on they made fun of her tomboy traits, teasing her about what they had praised her for previously. A rigid intolerance to humor and a serious defensive-mindedness developed in her which was crippling. No therapist could have known of this when he was launching her treatment. (I had known that she had left two therapists; but I did not know that this was because they had tried unwisely to treat lightly and teasingly the symptoms and fantasies about which she felt so deeply.) Nor could she have told anyone that she had quit her two previous efforts to find help because the two therapists had "bantered" in the dark, something which no therapist has any right to do. These two painful experiences with "humorous" therapists had made it almost impossible for her to try again, causing her to postpone definitive treatment for years and to bring into her third attempt even greater resistances and defensiveness. This is only one obvious example of the dangers inherent in the use of humor, and of how easy it is to misuse it.

Many argue that if humor is not aimed openly and directly at the patient, but rather at the patient's "opponents" in life, it communicates a "human touch" which can bridge gaps and bring the patient and the therapist closer together. There is some measure of truth in this. But this truth is limited by the fact that it is hard for the patient ever to feel sure that he is not in some unacknowledged way the butt of the humor. This may be only because he feels that he is suffering while the therapist is taking things gaily and lightly. It is never any fun to have a neurosis; nor is it ever fun to be in treatment. Consequently the therapist's humor, no matter how consciously well intended it may be, is usually perceived by the patient as heartless, cruel, and unfeeling.

While we may be masking our own hostilities with this humor, we silently pressure the patient to accept it without manifesting the justifiable resentment which he feels towards us for treating his suffering in so cavalier a fashion. The problem reminds one of the court jester, that mocking figure who had a special license to poke fun at the monarch, but with the threat of the king's wrath always hanging over his head. Here the patient is the monarch who may "lose his cool." Therefore even to poke fun secretly and gently may endanger the therapist's leverage. Two examples of mocking interpretations are reported in an article by Victor Rosen (3) (pages 719 and 720). In this account the disturbing intrusion of disguised hostility from both sides is evident, yet the immediate and remote consequences are not fully explored. This does not prove that the effects were either creative or destructive, but only that they are subtle, complex and often unpredictably dangerous.

The highly charged psychotherapeutic relationship is one of the most important relationships in the world, but also one of the most subtle and difficult. It puts demands on us as psychotherapists for which the human race is hardly ready. We have not reached a degree of maturity nor a quality of wisdom and generosity which justifies our attempting to play this role at all. Yet the pressing needs of sick patients force us to attempt it. As a result most of the technical devices of analytic therapy (such as the effort to preserve the analytic incognito and the separation between social and professional relationships) have as one of their central goals the protection of the patient from the frailties of the therapist. These devices provide generous and important contributions to the patient's welfare. We can leave their protection only with many precautions. Yet humor is a subtle way of circumventing these protective restrictions.

The frailty of human nature as manifested in the therapist takes many forms. The therapist, whether he seeks this or not, is placed automatically in a position of almost unquestioned authority to which he never is entitled. Against the therapist's frailties humor provides the patient with no protection, but leaves him even more vulnerable and more exposed. The therapist's position vis-à-vis the patient enables the therapist to project secretly and by substitutions many of his own unsolved problems. He transplants these unconsciously out of his own troubled past, and in doing so is likely to use the patient, and also the patient's family, as whipping boys, as surrogates for his own parents, siblings, spouse, old friends, etc.

The price of internal freedom (freedom from the internal tyranny of one's past) is that same vigilance which is required for the protection of our public liberties from external tyrannies. But humor blunts the vigilance of our self-observations and of our self-correcting efforts. We can maintain this indispensable vigilance only if we keep emotionally objective and uninvolved. Yet the sharing of humor automatically creates a powerful emotional involvement, just as does the sharing of grief. Thus it is easy to deceive ourselves about the fact that our manifestations of humor can be a form of self-display, of exhibitionism, of wooing. They say to a patient, "See how bright, and witty, and amusing, and charming, and delightful I can be." Consequently humor is especially tempting for the relatively constricted, sober, and humorless among therapists. It gives such a man an opportunity to parade himself as a wit before the eyes of his patients and, indirectly, of his colleagues. At the same time it is also a way of letting down the bars against his countertransference, as he smuggles humor in as a gesture of enticement. This is perhaps the most seductive form of transference wooing. Yet all the while, under such a barrage of self-gratifying and exhibitionistic humor from the therapist, the patient suffers silently. Whether he admits it or not, every patient is in pain; to have somebody viewing him and his pain with charm and easy humor may gratify the self-admiring therapist, but never the patient. And when the patient feels constrained to laugh along politely, he is merely trapped in a "laugh-in," because he is afraid to anger the therapist by not joining in. The secret devastation which goes on inside comes to light only much later.

The patient has no escape hatch. He is the therapist's captive audience, if the therapist is callous enough to misuse him in this way. Nor can the patient dare to say, "We are not amused," as did the good Queen Victoria when a court favorite attempted a lighthearted takeoff of some of her easily recognized mannerisms. In this respect humor in therapy is reminiscent of H. G. Wells' pithy comments on humor in the classroom, "Academic humor! Ugh!" There is nothing to which people are more sensitive than the toneless rejection of a witticism that has fallen flat. No matter how he feels, the patient has to pretend to be amused no matter what inner desperation he may be feeling. Humor then is a way of taking advantage of the patient. Over this desperation the therapist's humor runs a steamroller. I have picked up traces of the delayed bitter responses to the lighthearted or "bantering" approach of the therapist to the patient more often than I care to contemplate.

It is especially to the beginner that humor seems to be easier than any other way of introducing topics which are painful both to the patient and to the therapist. It is during the learning period that humor is most alluring and its use most dangerous. Yet for the beginner every one of these dangers and reservations is doubly loaded. Unless he is psychologically callous and unfit, the young psychiatrist, new to the therapeutic situation, takes up his responsibilities with a tense combination of masked terror and anger, from which humor is an escape or defense for him.

Over long years of experience supervising in private and hospital practice, analytically informed psychotherapists and young students of analysis, I have seen humor tried countless times. Yet in all of these many years I do not think that I can point to a single patient in whose treatment humor proved to be a safe, valuable, and necessary aid.

That even the therapist who defends the use of humor and "banter" feels some secret guilt about being "humorous" is proven by the fact that he almost never describes his own humor in his own accounts of therapeutic sessions. He forgets it, hides it, reports seriously what he had actually presented to the patient with "humor." Consequently the only way in which it would be possible for us to study a true sample of the use of humor in therapy would be by using videotape recordings of therapeutic and supervisory sessions.

Sometimes the joke is on the therapist, who cannot become or appear angry when the tables are turned. The therapist cannot always laugh along. If he does he will lose an invaluable opportunity to help the patient to gain more insight into the use of humor as a weapon. Clearly here the therapist walks a tightrope. There can be no rigid rules about how to handle this problem in treatment. Yet we hold always to the ultimate goal of facilitating the patient's free associations.

In this connection let me at once make it clear that much of this applies equally to that which the patient may smuggle past his own repressing mechanisms by using humor. Yet the effects on the patient of his own humor are not identical with the effects of the therapist's humor. I have seen patients speak the true word in jest quite freely, only to sit or lie in stunned silence as the realization slowly grew of the true implication of what they had just said.

In this connection the critical difference is that between smiling or laughing *with* someone (which never does any harm) or smiling and laughing *at* them. Therefore there is nothing in what I have written here which suggests that it is inappropriate or damaging to respond with appropriate amusement to a patient's spontaneous humor; particularly if such an interchange of humor enters into the therapeutic interchange only after the process is well along, and as one of the signs of improvement. Yet even here there is a hidden danger. The patient who has a gift for humor may offer humor not only as a screening device but also as a way of seducing his therapist out of his therapeutic role and into one of gay participation in fun.

Therefore I can qualify my reservations about the use of humor in therapy only to a limited extent and under special circumstances. It is never justifiable to make fun of patients or of their symptoms, no matter how strange or grotesque these may seem; nor of neurotogenic patterns of general behavior which are the symptomatic expressions of the underlying neurotic process. This serves only to increase the patient's pain, his resentment, and his defenses. On the other hand as a patient gradually achieves a progressively deeper self-understanding, then gentle and sympathetic humor can help the patient to mobilize his determination to utilize his new insights to that he can limit, control, and guide the symptomatic expression of that which remains of the neurotic process. In other words as insight helps the patient to emerge from domination by his own unconscious processes, the incorporation of these new insights into new conscious controls can sometimes be assisted by the light touch, but only then.

Certainly in the hands of a senior therapist humor can at such times be a safe and effective tool. Yet I am not ready to accept even so limited a claim without at least one serious reservation. What the senior does the junior soon will imitate. In fact every senior, whether or not he has formal status as a teacher, provides a pattern which younger men will try to imitate. So even if it could be demonstrated beyond question that the use of humor *late* in therapy is safe in the hands of the experienced, how can the inexperienced be dissuaded from imitating too early so easy and seductive and self-gratifying a device?

Humor has its place in life. Let us keep it there, by acknowledging that one place where it has a very limited role, if any, is in psychotherapy.

Bibliography

1. Grotjahn, Martin: *Beyond Laughter.* New York: McGraw-Hill, 1957, p. 285.
2. Kubie, L. S.: Some Aspects of the Significance to Psychoanalysis of the Exposure of a Patient to the Televised Audio-Visual Reproduction of his Activities. *Journal of*

Nervous and Mental Diseases, Vol. 148, No. 4, April 1969, pp. 301–309.

3. Rosen, Victor: Varieties of Comic Caricature, and Their Relationship to Obsessive Compulsive Phenomena. *Journal American Psychoanalytic Association,* Vol. XI, No. 4, 1963, pp. 704–724.

9/

"Gay" Jocularity
of the Homosexual

Lilla Veszy-Wagner, Ph.D.

*The accusation that wo-
men lack a sense of humor is posed mainly by
homosexuals.*

There are two types of homo-
sexual jokes. One Martin Grotjahn speaks of in his book
Beyond Laughter. This is the joke in which heterosexual men
"kid" the homosexuals and thus defend themselves against
homosexuality while at the same time enjoying it. The other
type of joke is one in which homosexuals laugh at the expense
of women without wanting to stimulate them. (Freud also
mentions the situation of the all male, but heterosexual, stag
parties where the latent homosexuality did not become
obvious to him until his book about group psychology.) In
looking at homosexual jokes, I understand why "the twain
shall never meet" as far as women and homosexual men are
concerned. They mutually find each other's jokes inane or
meaningless. Women in particular lack true understanding of
the homosexual's humor or the misogynist's jokes (the latter is
a euphemism for the latent homosexuals). Characteristically,

homosexuals do not make jokes about themselves or about heterosexual men, and it is no wonder that their aggressively obscene jokes directed against females do not amuse us women much. No group likes to be made fun of by an outsider who does not belong.

When first treating homosexuals I felt nonplussed about what they called humor. Next I felt dense, until I learned to decipher the humor analytically. Grotjahn finds "kidding" in homosexual jokes "a lower form of having fun." I must confess that at first I thought homosexuals only to be tedious and inane. However, not wanting to be a lady who protests too much, and trained to spot all unpleasant aspects of my countertransference, I tried to resurrect even the venerable ghost of penis-envy so that I might understand my homosexual patients; all to no avail. I remained unable to envy the male homosexual.

The "kidder," according to Martin Grotjahn, is allowed to attack, but he does not expect the attacked to hit back. This is similar to the public attitude regarding the Royal Family in England. In the name of enlightened liberty the wielders of the mass media do not think that it is in bad taste to attack the Queen's family jokingly, but it would be in very bad taste indeed if the Queen were to retaliate. Similarly, to be serious is in the worst taste, according to the homosexual creed. In *The Picture of Dorian Gray* Oscar Wilde said of a woman, "She was conversing in that intensively earnest manner which is the one unpardonable sin." The spoilsport is more passionately hated even than the "kidder." We analysts are so often accused of being spoilsports. It is never the "counterkidder" who is able to disarm the "kidder." But the analyst tolerant of homosexual humor can overcome the resistance of the kidder.

The hidden meaning of homosexual jocularity becomes understandable by the outsider, when it is recognized that the humor rests on two false premises: one, that women are by nature lesbians; the other, that women really do not appeal to men. The male homosexual suspects a lesbian relationship in every friendship between women. This would vindicate him, proving that women are not "better." They only give themselves airs. Conversely, this may be also regarded as an attempt by the male homosexual to make the female more like himself.

The accusation that women lack a sense of humor is posed mainly by homosexuals. There are, roughly, three kinds of laughter. Laughing *with* somebody is friendly and exuberant. Snickering brings viciousness into the fun. Giggling, which seems to contain both exuberance and viciousness, in fact loses meaning altogether. This is what makes some children's jokes and riddles insufferable. Preadolescent girls giggle, boys roar or hoot with laughter. Both are normal expressions of their exuberance and respective reaction to things which they guess but do not know, or have not yet digested. Both young and old homosexuals giggle to express viciousness and simulate exuberance. That is the reason why they call themselves "gay" but are called by others "queer." It is immaterial what newer slang words have been added to these; there is certainly a two-pronged meaning, a paradox in all of them. One cannot really be both gay and at the same time also withdrawn from other people in a furtive and eccentric way. In English language usage we distinguish between funny—ha ha—and funny—peculiar. What homosexuals think is funny is "The Woman" and also the fact that there are two sexes. Gay men are deathly afraid of the other sex and therefore try to devalue it by denial and laughter.

Clinical observations show that homosexuals feel bewilderment, and fall either into rage or depression if one does not share their merriment. One of my homosexual patients, who felt that he could only confide in me if he regarded me as an "honorary male homosexual," was irritated when I did not laugh at his joking.

The homosexual's defensive fantasy is revealed in some cartoons showing an immensely large woman towering over a diminutive man. A favorite Kipling quotation says that the female of the species is more deadly than the male. We must not forget that we are dealing with a grown-up baby who feels tiny and has forgotten to love.

It is not the homosexual's differences of sensitivity to humor which makes it so difficult to understand his jokes. Rather it is difficult to understand them because there is a joke within the joke. This joke is the homosexual's firm belief in the woman's phallicity. The homosexual assumes that everybody knows about the phallus of women, hence nobody needs to contradict it. Without recognition of this key belief the homosexual joke is undecipherable.

Perhaps analysts are the only persons in a position to understand the unhappy jocularity of the homosexual who asks for Mother to sanction his hostile attacks upon her. The homosexual suspects that all women are actually secret lesbians who cannot love men. This then is the final proof of the homosexual's deepest suspicion that mothers cannot love their sons. In order to respond to the jocularity of the homosexual we have to learn to decipher the hidden meaning of his jokes. However, we can easily be caught in a dilemma: If we don't appreciate it, we are resented as spoilsports. If we do respond with laughter, we are hailed as fellow-conspirators. There remains only one way to manage the joke of the homosexual in therapy. We can interpret it. Freud never advised against "chiming in" with a patient's joke. But he did advise interpreting at the right time and avoiding the untoward alliance with the patient leading to fraternization.

I do not see that we could do more with the homosexual joke than interpret it as Freud advises. Of course, we must prevent ourselves from acting on our natural or defensive aversion. We must be able to commiserate with the homosexual patient for his plight, without condescension. The understanding of the homosexual joke in therapy is expressed by the analyst in the correctness of his interpretation and not by his laughter.

10/

Grave Humor

Robert E. Litman, M.D.

*I honor Martin Grotjahn
as a teacher and as a psychoanalyst.*

Freud called it "gallows humor" or graveyard humor. Humor on sex or aging and retirement is tolerable, but how can death be funny? Martin Grotjahn asked that question in 1964 when he reviewed the film *Doctor Strangelove* for the *New York Times*. (4) He reported feeling fascinated, horrified, petrified by the images of world destruction, and while the young people laughed around him, he felt more and more alienated. Each generation, he decided, has to come to terms with its own version of the graveyard. Death is always with us; creative art helps us know it, live with it and even laugh at it. And this is not a recent development. As Dag Hammarskjöld wrote in his diary, "In the old days, death was always one of the party."

For twenty years Martin Grotjahn has been demonstrating to all of us the essence of what psychoanalysis has to offer. What I learned from him first and foremost, is the overwhelming importance for humans of the symbol. The first time I heard him talk, twenty years ago, he gave a paper titled "About the Representation of Death in the Art of Antiquity and in the Unconscious of Modern Men." (2) He said that the symbol, and especially the world of art, stands between our unconscious and our world of reality. He talked about the relationship of death to the creative urge. Progress toward maturity is related to problems of life. Progress toward wisdom is related to the problems of death.

My experience has been with depressed people and with efforts to forestall and prevent deadly acts and accidents. A recurring problem concerns the role of humor. Does humor tend to relieve depression or prevent self-destruction? In what manner or by what means can humor ward off death?

In the book *Beyond Laughter* (3) Martin Grotjahn says, "Wit is related to aggression, hostility and sadism; humor is related to depression, narcissism and masochism. Wit finds its psychomotor expression in laughter; humor in the smile." This inquiry is directed toward humor in its relationship to masochism and depression.

I have mixed feelings about laughter. If you, like me, have at some time been the object of laughter, you know how terribly destructive it can be. Yet laughter is highly valued as a universal human mode for discharging aggressive tension in groups. Please permit me a pair of wild ethological speculations. I wish to advance the theory that the primal laughter was part of a shared triumphant victory celebration when the early ape-men devoured their enemies. Civilization has only partially repressed and disguised that cannibalism. In celebrating the symbolic destruction of others, laughter is unifying; it brings people together.

By contrast, the smile is individualistic. We know the smile develops instinctively, early in infancy as a human recognition response. As another wild ethological speculation, I have a hunch that in the early development of man, the smile was useful as a turn-off signal for aggression, a sign of submission, and therefore, an inhibitor of violence. Modern men still use the smile to signal peaceful intentions when meeting strangers.

Humor is associated with feelings of relief. When those of us who are inclined toward masochism and depression see someone in trouble, we feel sorry for him. We feel a need to rescue him. Then, if we suddenly realize that we misunderstood the situation—the danger is not so pressing and no special action is needed after all—the relief is experienced as humor.

Let me illustrate with two examples from Shakespeare. Mercutio senses that he is fatally wounded and hastily summons a surgeon. Romeo says, "The hurt cannot be much." Mercutio responds, "No 'tis not so deep as a well nor so wide as a church door, but 'tis enough, 'twill serve. Ask for me tomorrow and you shall find me a grave man." Implication: I'm a goner, but save your pity. In Shakespeare's farewell play, *The Tempest*, Prospero, having confused and defeated his enemies, arranges his daughter's marriage, gives up his magic books and spirit servants, and retires to his native city, Milan "where every third thought shall be my grave." Were these Shakespeare's thoughts about his own retirement full of humor and success?

Allow me to restate the psychoanalytic understanding of humor. Humor is related to relief. It saves on pity. Brevity is essential. To be constantly laughing, smiling even, would be like an unending dream or a continuous fantasy and it would approach insanity. Indeed, inappropriate laughter and inappropriate smiling are symptoms of certain types of psychoses.

Humor is related to minor regressions such as sleep, dreams, fantasies, vacations, and coffee breaks. These interrupt the ongoing goal-directed acts and we allow our unconscious selves a little freedom. Then we come back to the world beyond laughter to resume and continue our lives, possibly in more creative and artistic ways. Note the difference between artistic creation and humor. The artistic involves us and increases tension, the humorous distances us and decreases tension.

In another context, commenting on the theater, Martin Grotjahn pointed out that we consider comedy as a low form of theater and tragedy the highest form of esthetic experience. The sadness of true and great art represents the symbiosis of life and death in harmony, while we see more plainly that humor denies both the harmony and the reality.

This is illustrated by the humorist Lenny Bruce discussing the H-bomb:

Well, it's a little embarrassing. You see seventeen thousand students marched down to the White House and Lyndon Johnson was left holding the bag.

"Mr. Johnson we're seventeen thousand students who have marched from Annapolis and we demand to see the bomb."

"Ah'd like to see it myself, son."

"Come on, now. Let's see the bomb. We're not gonna hurt anybody. We just want to take a few pictures, then we'll protest and that's it."

"Son, you're gonna think this is a lot of horseshit, but there never was a bomb. Them Hebe Hollywood writers made up the idea and they spread it around and everybody got afraid of this damn bomb story, but there is no bomb, just something we keep in the White House garage. We spent three million dollars on it and once we got it started, it just made a lot of noise and smelled up the whole house so we haven't fooled with it since."

"Now wait a minute. You see, I led the march and I've got seventeen thousand students that are protesting the bomb; don't tell me there's no bomb."

"Son, ah'd like to help you if I could, if I had a bomb."

"But what am I gonna tell all those poor kids out there—that there's no bomb?"

"The only thing that did work out was the button."

"What button?"

"The button that the madmen are always gonna push."

"That's what the bomb is—a button?"

"Yes, it's a button."

"Well, goddamn it, give me the button then."

"Can't do that, son, it's on a boy scout's fly and sometimes, somewhere a fag scoutmaster's gonna blow up the world." (1)

I have to admit that I , too, think that's funny. Those other madmen may blow up the world, but we crazy band of humorists will survive.

No, we won't. Not by laughing. Recently the Suicide Prevention Center of Los Angeles held a colloquium on "Violence." Dr. Jerome Frank discussed nuclear war and possibilities for avoiding it. He is a man of humor, but that talk was altogether serious. A discussant who tried to be funny sounded weird.

In real experience, suicide is remarkably unfunny. Suicidal people seem to have lost the capacity to feel humor. My colleague, Janet Green, and I have analyzed one thousand suicide notes which were the last messages from approximately three thousand consecutive Los Angeles suicides. The most common statements in suicide notes are "I'm sorry," "Forgive me," and "I love you." About one third give references to interpersonal relationships as something of an explanation for the suicide. Some statements are specific. "I can't live without you" (a certain person) is found in fourteen per cent of the notes. About nine per cent contain hostile, angry feelings. "I hate you." "You ruined my life." "Thanks for making me miserable." About seven per cent state "It's better this way." "I really want to die." About five per cent explain that they don't want to be any more burden or trouble to other people. About one third are more or less related to the person himself. For instance, fifteen per cent of the notes state "I can't live with this physical pain." Another five per cent say "I'm tired, worn out," and another ten per cent say "I just can't take it anymore, I'm a failure." About two per cent of the notes mention religion specifically, usually something about "God will forgive me." About three per cent of the notes consist of one word: "Good-bye." One third of the notes are not particularly addressed to other people nor are they explanatory about the feelings of the writers, but they simply consist of instructions: "Take good care of Sally." "My car is across the street." "Police, this is a suicide." Traces of what might be called humor were found in less than one per cent.

Let me present what might be called humor in suicide notes. From a forty-seven-year-old female, "I guess I should say stop the world, I want to get off. Please send my clothes to Gertrude. I just love you all too much to go on. You know what they say, Jack, the loss of a wife is like a sharp pain in the elbow. Soon over—so bye now. Love. Oh yes, I am in the garage."

From a forty-two-year-old male, who had been in Los Angeles for only a month, "Now is the time to go. The last meal has been eaten, the last girl has been kissed. I have sufficiently broken the bonds of love that I hardly will be missed. I don't know where I'm going, but I know that I must go, to somewhere else or nowhere. In a little while, I'll know." Then the date.

A forty-two-year-old male had been disposing of his belongings. He had a chronic kidney ailment. He slashed himself and bled to death. Note: "Please excuse the incarnadine appearance of the shower. I trust it will wash away easily. Wish I could say the same for my carcass."

The last is by a forty-year-old male who shot himself with a rifle he bought that morning. To Gilbert: "Please help my wife and keep my mother and family from upsetting her. My best to you and yours. P.S. Uncle, I'll save you a good spot, O.K.? P.P.S. My thanks to Dr. ——— of Encino. Tell him not to forget, you can't win them all, even if you are the best."

It has been suggested that true humorists find it impossible to commit suicide, even though they are essentially depressed and masochistic. This is the way Dorothy Parker put it in a poem.

> Razors pain you
> Rivers are damp,
> Acids stain you
> And drugs cause cramp.
> Guns aren't lawful
> Nooses give,
> Gas smells awful
> You might as well live.   (6)

There is some confirming evidence for the theory. Suicidal persons tend to be activists and "implementers," that means they are dissatisfied, impatient and all involved in some single issue which to them has life or death importance. Humor is an antidote to involvement and action. Humor makes for distance, detachment, nonparticipation and inaction. In theory, violent men, heroes, revolutionaries, assassins and suicides lack humor, although their lives may well be faithful, true and tragic.

But life is too complex for theories. The following paragraph is from a successful humorous novel by a talented young writer who later destroyed himself.

The dead, Roberts mused, what could you say for the dead of this war? What could you *really* say? Well, there were a lot of things you could say automatically and without thought, but they were all the wrong things; and just this once, just this one war, anyhow, let us try to say true things about the dead. Begin by cancelling the phrase "our honored dead"; for that is not true— we forget them, we do not honor them but in rhetoric, and the phrase is the badge of those who want something of the dead. If the dead of this war must have a mutual encomium, let it be "poor dead bastards." There is at least a little humanity in that. And let us not say of them this time "they gave their lives" for something or other; for certainly there was nothing voluntary in their dying. And neither is it fair to speak of "dead heroes" for not at all necessarily does the fact of death include the fact of heroism. Some of these dead were shining youths, scornful of the sanctity of their own lives, who lived daily with terror rarefied by inevitability and died with a flawless gesture of self-immolation; and others died as a result of injuries sustained in falling through a privy. But, thought Roberts, if they did not live equally, they are everyone equally dead. And you could say this affirmative thing of all; that in a war of terrifying consequence and overwhelming agony, they participated one hundred per cent. (5)

I can report to you from the Suicide Prevention Center that in dealing therapeutically on the telephone with suicidal strangers, humor is totally inappropriate. Those of our patients who are seriously suicidal respond to humor by hanging up. Humorous feelings stirred up in the emergency telephone therapist may correctly mirror the patient's low potential for violence; but with inexperienced therapists, humor more often stems from denial and false relief and a demand for distortion of the facts of death and violence. Better to encounter that suicidal stranger as a serious and creative actor in his tragic drama.

Recently, I tried to get an informal consultation from Martin Grotjahn. The patient was a businessman involved in a floundering publishing business which he idealized, as he had his mother. He was growing more and more depressed. Despite his efforts, he could not maintain the business both pure and successful. I said to Grotjahn, "He knows that the business is his mother, but how can I explain to him that his mother is a whore? Grotjahn, what would you do if I told you your mother is a whore?" And he thought for a moment and replied slyly, "I have suspected it all along." That is humor. But it did not help me with my patient, except as reassurance—"the problem isn't serious."

My first encounter with Dr. Grotjahn was about twenty years ago. We met for a consultation. I needed help and he participated one hundred per cent. The patient, poor woman, had been hospitalized many times and had received more than six hundred electric shock treatments for schizophrenia, which had become obvious after her marriage. Grotjahn had reviewed this case before, when it became apparent that the efforts of previous psychiatrists were unsuccessful. Now he asked me, "Litman, why do you want to take on this terrible situation?" I said, "I'm new in practice, Dr. Grotjahn, I need the money and I want to learn about schizophrenia." "OK," he said, "but what do you want from me?" "Well," I replied, ingenuously, "tell me what to do." So he told me. "You must become another schizophrenic in this family of psychotics." "Oh, I will," I promised, "what else?" "Well," he said, "it's not fair for the husband to have a schizophrenic wife; you'll have to arrange for a divorce." "Yes," I said, taking notes, "arrange a divorce." "And furthermore," he continued, "nobody has ever loved this woman except her father and he is the only one that loves her now. You should arrange for her to live with her father. Don't worry about incest, that won't hurt her at all." And I wrote down, "OK incest." Then I said, "But Grotjahn, her mother won't permit that." And he said, "Get rid of her mother." "But how will I do that?" "How? What do I care how. Kill her! Yah, hang her upside down from a hook and cut her throat and let her bleed to death in a bucket!" "But, Grotjahn, I can't do that. You don't understand America." "Litman, you don't understand schizophrenia!"

That was the best consultation I have ever had. It raised my tension, punctured my narcissism and brought me face to face with symbolic reality and it guided me to a successful result in this particular case. Told twenty years later with the knowledge of a happy ending, the story seems funny, but in fact, the consultation was in no way humorous, although it was aggressive, witty, dramatic and highly symbolic. More than a consultation, it was a work of art.

Essentially, the goal of humor and of art is to give pleasure. I have raised the issue of the therapeutic value of humor. Suicidal persons lack humor. It may well be advisable to stress the development of humor as one of the goals in the long-range rehabilitation therapy of depressed and suicidal patients. However, during an acute destructive crisis, intervention by humor is usually inappropriate. Better is the artistic encounter and participation with the patient in his symbolic tragedy. In psychotherapy and education, as in entertainment, the essence of humor is in the timing. And perfect timing turns humor into art.

Bibliography

1. Bruce, Lenny: *How to Talk Dirty and Influence People.* Chicago: Playboy Press, Inc., 1963.

2. Grotjahn, Martin: About the representation of death in the art of antiquity and in the unconscious of modern men. In: *Psychoanalysis and Culture.* New York: International Universities Press, Inc., 1951.

3. Grotjahn, Martin: *Beyond Laughter.* New York: McGraw-Hill, 1957.

4. Grotjahn, Martin: A psychiatrist's strange love for *Dr. Strangelove:* the strange new humor of a brave new world. *New York Times,* February 20, 1964.

5. Heggen, Thomas: *Mister Roberts.* New York: Pocket Books, Inc., 1946.

6. Parker, Dorothy: Enough Rope. *Poems by Dorothy Parker.* New York: Boni and Liveright, 1926.

11/

Young Freud as a Poet

Alexander S. Rogawski, M.D.

Interesting would be a comparison of the effects of the ascetic adolescence of Freud's generation with the hedonistic orientation of today's youth whose sexual attitudes, at least in part, became possible as a result of the impact of Freud's work.

Martin Grotjahn shares with Freud the love of humor and the desire to unravel laughter's significance for the intellectual, emotional and communicating life of man. For many years he has also diligently hunted for manuscripts and letters written by the founder of psychoanalysis in the hope of illuminating the making of a creative genius.

A little known poem which Freud composed in his adolescence and which was recently discovered in a collection of letters and postcards written to Edward Silberstein, a close friend of the secondary school years (12), may provide some insight into the functions of wit as well as open a view on Freud's adolescent years.

Young Freud as a Poet

Twice during his lifetime Freud destroyed all of his correspondence, notes, diaries, drafts and manuscripts to protect his private life from the curiosity of posterity. The first time was in 1885. He was almost twenty-nine years old and was about to leave his hospital quarters for a homeless existence. He needed to rid himself from the accumulated jottings of the past and was disturbed by the thought of "who might come by the old papers." (10) In a humorous letter to his betrothed, Martha Bernays, he predicted accurately that as yet unborn future biographers would deplore his action, "Let the biographers chafe; we won't make it too easy for them. Let each one of them believe he is right in his 'Conception of the Development of the Hero'; even now I enjoy the thought of how they will go astray." For this reason letters from periods preceding the extensive correspondence with Martha which began on June 15, 1882, on the eve of their engagement, are exceedingly rare.

The Silberstein correspondence extended from 1871, when Freud was only fifteen years old until 1881, shortly before Freud met his bride. It consists of over fifty-five pieces of mail, letters and postcards, of which thirty-three are written in German, twenty-two in poor Spanish and some partly in German and partly in Spanish. (12)

Years later in a letter to Martha, Freud reported that he had just been visited by Silberstein who had been his friend "at a time when friendship is entertained not just for pleasure or because it offers practical advantages but when a friend is needed to share life with." (8) (Author's translation.)

Freud continues in the letter, "We used to spend every hour of the day together and we created our own private mythology and secret names which we lifted from a speech by the great Cervantes. In our Spanish primer we found a humorous philosophical dialogue between two dogs which lie peacefully in front of the entrance to a hospital and we appropriated their names for ourselves. He was called Berganza and I myself Cipio in our written as well as in our oral communications. How often did I write to him: 'Querido Berganza' and than I signed with 'Tu fidel Cipio, pere en el hospital de Sevilla.' We formed a strange scholarly society, the Academia Castellana, we compiled a large number of funny writings which must still be somewhere among my old papers, we shared our frugal suppers and we were never bored in each other's company. Intellectually he had no high aspirations; he stayed within the area of being human; his outlook, his humor, all were bourgeois and somewhat prosaic." (8)

The poem which was found among the letters to Silberstein is entitled "Hochzeitscarmen" or "Wedding Song" since *carmen* is the Latin word for song. It was enclosed in a letter dated October 2, 1875, written by Freud when he was nineteen years old. It seemed occasioned by the marriage of a young unnamed woman to a Mr. Rosenzweig. The couple's relationship to Freud and his friend is not specified.

Hochzeitscarmen (Wedding Song)

by a Homerian of the Ac. Esp. (d.h. Sigmund Freud)

Sing to me, Muse, the glory of the Ichthyosauri
  communes,
Once so powerful in the Lias and in other
  formations,
Which had been a splendid model to the
  Academia,

So that a prize was set on their appearance.
Yet they were smothered by the weight of the
    subsequent chalk,   5
Until it too crumbled to pieces—since nothing
    on earth is eternal.
Cherish such memories, Muse, and relish the
    news,
Which was received with enthusiasm just now
    red hot from a friend.
But, how shall I begin—ignorant of the Lesbian
    lute
To praise the one—Helen in beauty—who
    irresistibly   10
Conquers the hearts of men, surrenders
    herself to sighs?
Her figure was not too tall, she did not
    resemble the poplar
which in blameless growth strives straight
    toward heaven
Nor to the pine tree or fir, adornment of
    Nordish forests,
Nor to the Lebanon's cedar, the classical tree
    of the Jews,   15
But to the highest of forms, the ideal of
    configurations,—
Globe-like did she appear, deliciously fully
    rounded
Round in the face with intelligent sparkling
    eyes
Round the body's contour, and if the poet is
    granted
To thrust his perceptive eye where common
    view is excluded   20
He cannot doubt that the roundness principle
    proves itself in the forms

Which to the fortunate husband the blessed
    evening reveals.
Envious and hatefilled people maintain that all
    Ichthyosauri
Which were thus named by Linné and by
    Jussieu the scholar,
Wander across this world supplied with a
    pumpkin-like head—   25
Though no mortal eye ever perceived this
    defect on Ichthyosauri
—except hairdressers perhaps—since
    glisteningly fell from the crown
And from the temples the head's waving ocean
    of hair
Now plaited in braids, now freely moved by
    the wind,
Now with the luster of suns, now dull as straw's
    color appearing   30
Beauty's exquisite ornament, envied in Madrid
    and Sevilla.
But, oh Muse, you must mourn the rapid
    passing of pages
And the hurrying mail which does not grant us
    to tarry
Nor to describe the brilliance and inner color
    of eyes
Which, whether gray or green no mortal can
    judge and decide   35
Nor the shape of the nose, of chin nor the ears'
    formation,
But with fleeting glance it bids you to survey
    the virgin
Resplendent who to become a housewife will
    now unite with the man.

But this doubt pray solve, Muse, since pressing
    it seems:
Scoffers, deriders, blasphemers, ignorant of
    indulgence   40
Momusses,* judges: such as would criticize
    children
Still in the mother's womb and unseen by
    anyone's eye
Frequently claim—may Zeus destroy them,
    avenger of evil—
That in the sunny body the spirit stirs only in
    dullness
That in the narrow brain a simple wit reigns
    without power   45
Confined by ribbons and bows and by
    possession of braids,
Never the eye reflected the rays of fine
    education,
Never did it light up grasping the spirit's
    powers,
Never with wondering gaze beheld it the
    depths of knowledge
Never wished it to look—like the eye of the
    burrowing mole.   50
Goddesses both, Minerva and Juno adorned
    the one
Who had been the only darling of smiling
    Aphrodite.
Muse, dissolve me those doubts, You know it
    better than others
You saw her go to school and listened in on
    her thoughts
You heard her mumble Gaul's tongue from a

*Mommus . . . Greek god of blame and mockery.

mouth proudly swelling   55
And all this science—as far as it's suited for girls
And is taught in her boarding school—she's
   got it, you know that.
You could not equal another quickly to her in
   skills
Rapidly grows from her hands the stocking in
   the clatter of needles
Eagerly does she wield the tool mending holes
   in dresses   60
Where the ferment of the pores permitted air's
   taking possession.
Cleverly does she dissect the herring and
   cleans it with water
Separates milk from the meat and serves the
   food at the table
Whatever she bakes is tasty, neither salt nor
   sugar are lacking
Not seasoning in the soups—so numerous are
   her skills.   65
Thus she needn't feel shame extending her
   hand to the youth
Who in Germany studied the art of acquiring
   money.
'Rose-branch' is his name since she blooms a
   rose on his branch.
May they be happy both—their bridal bed
   blessed and soft.
Both of unblemished lineage, radiant with
   beauty and riches.   70
May their home be filled with bliss, may the
   roast never want in the oven
May the steel-enforced safe be never without
   any papers

And may both bring to completion the
   predestination of life—
Like insects and like worms which populate
   this our world
Endowed with unhampered breathing and the
   ingestion of food   75
And never moved by the spirit—thus wishes
   the Academia.
                    (Translated from the German by
                    Alexander S. Rogawski, M.D.)

Freud's poem cannot be re-
garded a serious artistic production. It was never intended to
be one. It is clearly an in joke among friends.

Stanescu (12) remarks correctly
that the uninitiated reader would never be able to predict that
the poem's author would some day mature into an accomplished master of the German prose whose superb command
of the language enhanced the fascination of his scientific writings. (11) The poem is wordy, the witticisms are strained, the
sarcastic descriptions of the couple to be joined in marriage
are merciless. There are many obscure allusions so typical for
communications between adolescents. They succeed in keeping the outsider in the dark as to their correct meaning.

The limping hexameters par-
odying a Homeric epic—and Freud refers to himself in the
subtitle as a "Homerian of the Spanish Academy"—lend themselves easily to sarcastic and pompous gravity. Austrian and
German students educated in Roman and Greek classics used
this form often to deride people, occasions and institutions.

A long "epic" poem making
fun of a high school teacher, a Professor Meyer, and appropriately called the "Meyeriad," was an immensely popular paper-
back in my student days in the Twenties.

Alexander S. Rogawski

A brief epilogue to the poem contributes little toward its clarification. Freud states that only the special occasion of the "marriage of a principle" could cause him to expose himself to the heavy strain of poetic creation. The two friends had vowed to compose a poem only if important occasions such as the present one would arise. Fortunately, such disturbing events occurred only rarely.

What Freud means by "principle" is not entirely clear. In this poem "principle" refers to the principle of roundness "the highest of forms—the ideal of configurations." It seems that the bride in question was somewhat plump and therefore rated the following description in the poem:

> Her figure was not too tall, she did not resemble the
>   poplar
> Which in blameless growth strives straight towards
>   heaven
> Nor the pine tree or fir, adornment of Nordish
>   forests,
> Nor to the Lebanon's cedar, the classical tree of the
>   Jews,
> But to the highest of forms, the ideal of
>   configurations,—
> Globe-like did she appear, deliciously fully rounded
> Round in the face with intelligent sparkling eyes
> Round the body's contour, and if the poet is granted
> To thrust his perceptive eye where common view is
>   excluded
> He cannot doubt that the roundness principle
>   proves itself in the forms
> Which to the fortunate husband the blessed
>   evening reveals.

> (Lines 12–22)

This excerpt is rather typical of the style and general attitude of the poem. It is, however, by no means the only sarcastic reference to the marrying couple.

Most of the poem, sixty-five of the seventy-six lines, are devoted to the bride. The bridegroom is allotted merely three lines in which—with obvious condescension—he is described as a youth.

Who in Germany studied the art of acquiring
   money.
'Rose-branch' is his name since she blooms a rose
   on his branch.

(Lines 67 and 68)

The poem begins with an appeal to the muse traditional in Greek and Roman epics. The poet urges her to sing of the glory of the "Ichthyosauri communes." It is not clear why he refers to the couple as a pair of prehistoric animals though Stanescu surmises that Freud tried in this way to symbolize their conservative and philistine attitudes. (12).

After describing the bride and especially her roundness Freud states that some envious and hate-filled people claim that Ichthyosauri have pumpkinlike heads. This cannot be ascertained—except perhaps by the hairdresser—since the bride's head is completely covered with a mess of hair. Her other facial features Freud finds nondescript.

With feigned indignation Freud turns against "scoffers, deriders, blasphemers, ignorant of indulgence" who allege that only a dull spirit stirs in "the sunny body" and

That in the narrow brain a simple wit reigns without
   power

Confined by ribbons and bows and by possession of
   braids,
Never the eye reflected the rays of fine education,
Never did it light up grasping the spirit's powers,
Never with wondering gaze beheld it the depths of
   knowledge,
Never wished it to look—like the eye of a burrowing
   mole.
                                        (Lines 45–50)

         In biting sarcasm Freud urges
the muse to dispel such allegations. The muse should know
better. She saw the bride attend school and mumble in French.
The girl must have acquired some knowledge of science

   . . . as far as it's suited for girls and is taught in her
   boarding school . . .
                        (Lines 56 and 57)

         Only the lady's domestic skills
rate a few words of praise—and even these are not without
disdain.

         In the final verses the couple is
wished happiness, a soft and blessed bridal bed, an oven with
an ever-present roast in it and a steel-enforced safe always
filled with valuable papers.

And may both bring to completion the
   predestination of life—
Like insects and like worms which populate this our
   world
Endowed with unhampered breathing and the
   ingestion of food
And never moved by the spirit—thus wishes the
   Academia.
                              (Lines 73–76)

                                              •

Thus the poem. The reader is left wondering what might have caused young Freud to engage in this unkind exercise of scathing mockery. Why has the young lady especially become the victim of his unbridled sarcasm? Grotjahn notes, "Aggressive tendencies in the examples |of jokes| quoted by Freud seem to be directed with special intensity against wives or brides, a little less frequently against bridegrooms and parents." (9)

In our search for an explanation, let us assemble some data known about this period of Freud's life.

Freud was nineteen years old when he composed the poem. Two years before he had registered, with considerable ambivalence, in the Medical School of Vienna University. "Neither at that time nor indeed in my later life did I feel any particular predilection for the career of a doctor." (7) His indecision found expression in the diffuse character of his studies. He plunged "in youthful eagerness" into various branches of science only to find himself unsuited for them by temperament or inclination. He had not yet settled down in physiology, which at that time consisted mostly of histology. This happened in the following year when, under the influence of the revered teacher Ernst Bruecke, he engaged in pure research and remained with it for six years (1876–1882), delaying his graduation from medical school by three years.

Biographer Ernest Jones explains Freud's concentration on concrete and factual research as "an effort to counteract a strong pull towards speculation and ruthlessly checked it." (10)

We may suspect that the intense involvement with studies and research served also some other defensive functions, especially when we review the adolescent Freud's relations to women which appear surprisingly wanting.

At the age of sixteen Freud had returned for the first time to the place of his birth, Pribor in Moravia, which he and his family had left when he was but three years old. (8, Letter #263) He stayed with old friends of his parents, the Fluss family, who had a daughter Gisela, a year younger than himself.

What happened during this visit was revealed in a beautiful essay in which Freud allegedly reported on the analysis of a screen memory of one of his patients. (2) Bernfeld established beyond any doubt that the anonymous patient was none other than Freud himself, even though some minor dates had been changed to conceal the true identity. Here is Freud speaking through his stand-in: "I was seventeen, and in the family where I was staying there was a daughter of fifteen, with whom I immediately fell in love. It was my first puppy-love and sufficiently intense, but I kept it completely secret. After a few days the girl went off to her school (from which she too was home for the holidays) and it was this separation after such a short acquaintance that brought my longings to a really high pitch. I passed many hours in solitary walks through the lovely woods that I had found once more and I spent my time building castles in the air." (5)

Freud regretted that his family had moved away from the small town. If they had stayed he would not have become distracted by intellectual pursuits. He would have become interested in business and would have been able to marry the young lady.

After this painful disappointment he protected himself from similar temptations for ten years. Not until 1882 did he allow himself to fall in love again, this time with Martha Bernays, his wife-to-be. Once again it was love at first sight. Yet even then Freud did not get married until after four years of separation, after writing over nine hundred letters to his betrothed, and after passing his thirtieth birthday.

At the age of nineteen he spent the summer with his twenty-four-year-older half-brother Emanuel of Manchester, England. Freud's father and Emanuel had hoped that Sigmund would become attracted to Emanuel's daughter, Pauline, an eighteen-year-old girl who had been his playmate in his early years in Pribor. Their plan was that Freud would become interested in business, would give up his intellectual aspirations and settle in Manchester. But Freud foiled their scheme. He did not give the girl a tumble.

In the previously quoted analysis of the screen memory Freud explains "my bashfulness on the first opportunity, my indifference on the second" (2) by the need to maintain the repression of early forbidden wishes and rape fantasies concerning Pauline when they were both little children.

In his paper he muses, "You think to yourself: If I had married 'so-and-so' and behind this thought there is the impulse to imagine what 'being married' really means . . . The most seductive aspect of the whole subject for an idle young man is the imagining of the wedding night; who cares what comes afterwards. But this fantasy does not venture out into the light of day: the prevailing mood of modesty and respect for the girl keeps it suppressed. So it remains unconscious—" (4) (Author's translation)

The desire to imagine what happens on the wedding night breaks through in the poem in the whimsical reflection,

> . . . and if the poet is granted
> To thrust his perceptive eye where common view is
>   excluded
> He cannot doubt that the roundness principle
>   proves itself in the forms
> Which to the fortunate husband the blessed
>   evening reveals.
>
> (Lines 19–22)

These lines were written shortly after Freud had returned from Manchester, England, where he had so effectively suppressed awareness of young Pauline. Jones refers to this period in Freud's life as an "increased wave of sexual repression" and speculates whether it was "a contributory factor in his turning so sharply from the chances of worldly ambition and ease towards the cold flame of idealism that intellect promised." (10)

In the same year Freud's family moved to a larger flat in the Kaiser Josefstrasse but "the first-born son of a youthful mother" (8, Letter #263) still had to share cramped quarters with five young sisters. Sigmund was the only member in the family of eight who was granted a room all to himself. It was a small and narrow study, which in various writings is referred to as his "Cabinet."

Against the inevitable temptation of so much youthful femininity Freud protected himself with puritanical severity. He exercised strict censorship over the reading matter of his sisters and warned Anna against the writings of Balzac and Dumas when she was already fifteen. (1) He withdrew to his small study and buried himself in his books, even eating his evening meal alone so as not to lose any time from his studies. When Anna's piano practicing interfered with his concentration she had to give up the piano even though she had shown some musical talent.

His boyfriends came often to
visit but according to his oldest son Martin, "The presence of
five young women in the flat had not the slightest effect on
these young men: the girls never received even the suspicion
of a sidelong glance. These young men made straight for the
cabinet disappearing without trace to begin scientific discussions with Freud." (9)

This indicates that not only
Freud but also other young men of his circle and of similar
social and cultural background, kept away from young ladies
during their adolescence. They got involved in intense friendships with each other which often lasted for many years. Freud
himself remarked on the intensity of his friendships with men
(6, Letter#70). He ascribed it to his early relationship with John,
the one-year-older son of his half-brother, Emanuel, and considered it also a reaction to the death of a younger infant
brother which occurred before Freud himself had reached the
age of two.

His early personal history un-
questionably affected his behavior but we suspect that
socio-cultural factors exerted an important influence.

These young men attended all-
male secondary schools. They spent eight important years,
from ten to eighteen, together in small and stable classes and
became intimately acquainted with each other. The prolonged
isolation from girls, reinforced by the prevailing mores, pro-
moted the establishment of close and emotionally intense
male friendships. Freud's friendship with Silberstein was an
example of such a relationship and a precursor of many others
to follow throughout his life. The "Bund," a group of friends
who would meet regularly in their favorite coffeehouse, the
"committee" of early psychoanalytic disciples and other similar associations must have fulfilled needs which were created

during adolescence and which were apparently never entirely abandoned. These close associations protected the young men from anxieties aroused by the possibility of actual heterosexual involvement. But they had also a value of their own. They served unquestionably as an opportunity for sharing yearnings and apprehensions in mutual exchanges. In the lives of these young men their friendships became a cherished ingredient which they gave up only with great reluctance and deep sadness.

In the previously quoted letter to Martha Bernays, in which Freud reminisces about the times spent with Silberstein, he reports how his friend called his buddies together for a farewell party when the time had come for him to leave Vienna: "Silberstein, himself, with his good natured expression poured the beer from a barrel in order to conceal his emotion. Then while we were sitting together in a cafe and Rosanes [a Vienna surgeon and member of the group] was telling bad jokes, also only to prevent his sentimentality from overflowing, I was the first to break the ice and in the name of them all I made a speech in which I said he was taking with him my own youth, little realizing how true this was." (8, Letter #37)

After relating how he and his friend Silberstein kept up a correspondence, "Then you appeared on the scene and everything that came with you; a new friend, new struggles, new aims."

Youth for Freud and his friends was the period of their masculine associations. It came to an end when women entered their lives. No wonder that they tried to prolong their youth as long as they could and treated women, especially those who were desirous of marrying them, as if they were dangerous disturbers.

The wedding which gave birth to the poem had at least two effects on Freud: It stimulated sexual fantasies which at that particular time he tried mightily to suppress, and it created sadness in him because he sensed that such an event would some day set an end to cherished adolescent male friendships.

The unusually caustic and contemptuous tone of the poem may be recognized as Freud's attempt to mask and to defend himself against disturbing feelings. Like Rosanes at the farewell party, Freud tried to cover up with a "bad joke" his sentiments aroused by the realization that youth must end some day.

It would be most enticing to continue these considerations with an exploration and with some speculation how Freud's very prolonged adolescence influenced his thoughts and attitudes, his thinking on sexuality and his concepts of femininity. Equally interesting would be a comparison of the effects of the ascetic adolescence of Freud's generation with the hedonistic orientation of today's youth whose sexual attitudes, at least in part, became possible as a result of the impact of Freud's work. Such considerations are beyond the scope of the present paper. We shall be content if we have shown by way of Freud's poem how an adolescent employed witticism in the service of defense against threatening and undesired emotions.

Bibliography

1. Bernays-Freud, Anna: My Brother Sigmund Freud. In: *American Mercury,* November, 1940.

2. Bernfield, Siegfried: An Unknown Autobiographical Fragment by Freud—*The American Imago,* Vol. IV (1946); pp. 3–19. Reprinted in: *The Year Book of Psy-*

choanalysis, Lorand, Sandor (Ed.), Vol. 3. London: Imago Publishing Co., 1948, pp. 15–29.

3. Freud, Martin: Glory Reflected. *Sigmund Freud—Man and Father.* London: Angus & Robertson, 1957.

4. Freud, Sigmund: Ueber Deckerinnerungen (1899). In: *Gesammelte Werke,* Vol. 1. London: Imago Publishing Co., 1952.

5. Freud, Sigmund: Screen Memories, 1899. In: *Standard Edition,* Vol. 3, 1962, pp. 303–322. London: Hogarth Press, 1962.

6. Freud, Sigmund: *The Origins of Psychoanalysis.* Letters to Wilhelm Fliess, Drafts and Notes, 1887–1902. New York: Basic Books, Inc., 1954.

7. Freud, Sigmund: An Autobiographical Study. (1924) In: *Standard Edition,* Vol. 20, pp. 7–74. London: Hogarth Press, 1959.

8. Freud, Sigmund: *Letters of Sigmund Freud.* (Selected and edited by Ernst L. Freud) New York: Basic Books, Inc., 1960.

9. Grotjahn, Martin: *Beyond Laughter.* New York: McGraw–Hill, 1957.

10. Jones, Ernest: *The Life and Work of Sigmund Freud.* Vol. 1, New York: Basic Books, Inc., 1953.

11. Schoenau, Walter: *Sigmund Freud's Prosa. Literarische Elemente seines Stils.* Stuttgart: J. B. Metzler, 1968.

12. Stanescu, Heinz: Ein Gelegenheitsgedicht des jungen Sigmund Freud. In: *Deutsch fuer Auslaender.* Information fuer den Lehrer. January, 1967, pp. 13–18.

12/

A God Who Laughs

Carlo Weber, Ph.D.

*I enjoy Martin Grotjahn
immensely. The celebration of laughter is delicious
and I propose to enjoy it to the fullest.*

In the preface of his book,
Beyond Laughter, Martin Grotjahn writes that his book is, to
his own regret, not funny. (18) Laughter is not its aim, but its
by-product. And laughter has a tendency to disappear when
we try to explain it. I now feel constrained to repeat the same
sad warning here. What follows will, I am afraid, be a humorless paper about humor. I shall make no attempt to be funny,
at least not deliberately. And if it turns out that I am funny,
then that very fact may best illustrate the point I should like to
make: that man may often be funniest when he least means to
be.

The shocking presumption that
one would dare attempt to explain the laughter of the gods, of
all things, imposes yet a further dilemma. Laughter is, as
everyone from Freud to Grotjahn has insisted, an essentially
cruel enterprise, the mask of aggression, rendered socially
acceptable under the disguise of humor. Whether or not such

a thing as harmless wit can even exist is, at best, a moot point. Sophisticated observers decipher aggressive tendencies in what appear to be the most innocent of witticisms. The grounds for this interpretation lie in the fact that through time, the repressive forces of society have muted aggression from overt assault to wit. The assault is disguised in a clever joke, and the butt of the joke is the person attacked. If this is so, can we properly attribute such humor to God? Is the laughter of the gods only a jeering assault upon the ineptitude of man, who then becomes the butt of an incredibly cruel cosmic joke? The wolf, we know, shows its fangs to display its superiority to other animals; laughter is man's way of showing his superiority over other men. Does God then bare his teeth in cruel laughter?

To complicate the matter a bit further, we note that Bergson, in his classic but rather incomplete essay on comedy, insists that laughter cannot exist outside what is strictly human. "A landscape," he writes, "may be beautiful, charming, sublime, or insignificant and ugly—it will never be laughable. You can laugh at an animal, but only because you have detected in it some human attitude or expression. You may laugh at a hat; but what you are making fun of is not the piece of felt or straw, but the shape that man has given it, the human caprice whose mold it has assumed." (1) To lose one's humanness is to lose one's sense of laughter, with the restoration of the human comes the capacity to laugh. In this connotation we laugh with our human frailty, rather than at it. Preserving this restriction of the meaning of humor, psychotherapy, which is the eminently human enterprise, participates by that fact in the aesthetic tradition of comedy, not tragedy. And the psychotherapist, the healer, adorns himself with the comic, not the tragic mask, as he extends an invitation to the tragic face to smile. The playfulness of the Greek gods and goddesses, romping on Delphic heights, was an expression of their humanness, not their divinity; and so we could laugh with them. Homer nods and Zeus laughs; and our sense of kinship in human nature is ratified in laughter. If, then, such laughter is the property of the human, can one reasonably attribute it to God?

One usually poses rhetorical questions with the subtle confidence that the dilemma proposed will disintegrate in the face of the devastating argument to follow. Such, I am afraid, is not the case here. True to the nature of comedy, I shall make no attempt whatever to resolve the dilemma. I have no way of untwisting the riddle. Comedy creates riddles; it does not try to solve them. Comedy is the sound of the one hand clapping; attempts at solutions are tragic.

The fact is that there is an obvious historical relationship between the comic and the sacred. We rarely experience the need to laugh more than in church or at a solemn gathering. Every university graduate has had to struggle with the urge to laugh at graduation ceremonies. The ill-designed hat is more ludicrous in church than on the street. Our need to laugh is apparently greatest at the most sacred moments. For laughter is an escape from smug, pretentious bondage. Placed in bondage, we either submit to it, or laugh at it. So we must laugh at death and taxes, at momism and oedipal complexes, at funeral excesses, and even, sadly, at prospects of atomic annihilation, at whatever tragic invention becomes our jailer. Laughter tends to correct oppressive abuse and release our aggressions against the binding force.

One element of the dilemma suggests a starting point: The fact that man can laugh at all is rooted in his being human and finite. Together, we are the *Steppenwolf* (20), half man, half wolf, with roots in the mud and in the trees, head in the sky, and an inner face that smiles in return when we peer studiously into our mirrors. Man is, as human, essentially *incongruous*. We didn't invent this incongruity; we are at our best when we discover it. Laughter may be our only response to this puzzling, aggravating, frustrating incongruity, our most successful meeting with the chasm we see between divine possibilities and human realities. We stand and peer into the chasm, but we cannot bridge it. In the need to laugh at a solemn religious event, we may be responding in the only reasonable way to the basic incongruity of all: that the infinite is actually somehow involved with the finite, that God does somehow insert Himself into the cosmos of His own creation, and that the divine and the human are therefore both in contradiction and in union. If not the laughter of incongruity at such a thought, then the laughter of desperation. For that wedding of the divine and the human has got to be the greatest joke of all.

If this incarnation is the greatest joke, then there ought to be evidence in the sacred writings of a God who laughs. Unfortunately, as Grotjahn also notes (19), there are precious few examples of laughter in the scriptures. But where such examples are narrated, they occur with remarkable impact. The first book of the Old Testament, Genesis, is the book of beginnings; and in a manner that, I believe, is not simply coincidental, the book records, among other things, the beginning of laughter. Early in the narrative (11), God promises the aging Abraham, father of the race, the most cherished of Jewish possessions, a male heir. Upon receipt of this news, Abraham falls flat on his face in laughter, saying to himself, "Can a child be born to a man who is a hundred years old?" And when the promise is repeated to his wife, Sarah, she hides herself, and laughs, after the fashion of women, within herself. Possibly annoyed by this response, the Lord questions Abraham: "Why does your wife Sarah laugh? Is anything too hard for the Lord?" And because apparently nothing is too hard for the Lord, laughter is born. For in naming her son Isaac, Sarah called him laughter. And to bear witness, she announces; "God has made laughter for me. And everyone who hears will laugh with me. For who would have said that Sarah would suckle children. And yet, I have born to Abraham a son in his old age."

In the laughter of Abraham and Sarah, the incongruous gap between what is and what should be is first perceived. And for a moment, Abraham and Sarah feel superior to the Lord, and are convinced that the joke is on Him. They see the incongruity of the promise of a son with the harsh realities of old age. But when the incongruous becomes a palpable fact, the laughter of unbelief becomes the laughter of faith. Even more absurd than the promise, and then the fact of Isaac's birth is the event that follows. Having produced laughter in such a manner, the Lord subsequently commands Abraham to kill Isaac (12), that is, to destroy laughter. Again, Abraham is tempted to demur. This, even more than the promise, is a cruel joke. But incongruous and cruel as it seems to be, Abraham nonetheless prepares himself to carry it out. And when he holds the knife above Isaac's head, he places himself, as Kierkegaard observes, outside and beyond all moral norms. (25) He is either a murderer or a believer, or perhaps both. His dilemma can only be transcended, not resolved, by a perspective that is so far extrapolated beyond normal value systems that it must extend from infinity. At that point, Abraham is rescued from the irreconcilable. The Lord spares Isaac; laughter is preserved on the horns of a ram in a thicket. The ram that saves laughter may be a figure of our Steppenwolf, also a laughing being from another world. (20)

Comic heroes such as Abraham find themselves in such situations because comedy begins with the absurd and the inexplicable. And like faith, comedy tolerates the mysterious, the enigmatic. Dostoevsky begins with the ludicrous when he has old Karamazov sleep with Lizaveta who begets Smerdyakov, as much his son as the saintly Alyosha. In coming face to face with the absurd, the comic hero grows great. Don Quixote jousts with windmills, slaying them for his Dulcinea, perceives a lowly innkeeper as a king, and a barber's chafing basin as a knightly crown, and is mad to the degree of pouring curds over his head. He is absurd, a fool, a madman. But his absurdity is greatest reason, his foolishness ultimate wisdom, and in madness, he dies a saint. Reality is what we perceive it to be. But only the comic hero can live with penetrating misperception. The tragic hero cannot play with life; he must meet dilemmas, and pay the penalty for not being able to reconcile them. Thus, he must remain torn apart. The comic hero, with the agility of the clown, can be nimble and be quick—and can live with the contradictories. The guru, in Eastern ways of liberation, plays the same comic role, tricking the student into accepting himself and gaining mastery over the imaginary problem. (28) Perhaps the prototypes of the comic hero and heroine are aging Abraham and Sarah, who gave birth to laughter.

There are other examples of laughter in the Old Testament, most of them in the Psalms, where the aggressive component seems to loom large. In the second Pslam, we read that "He who sits in the heavens, laughs—and laughs in derision." And in the prophetic Passion Psalm, we read the line " . . . all they that see me, laugh me to scorn." (14)

In the New Testament, the same theme is extended in the person of Jesus, except that the laugh has become more of a smile. For Jesus is the comic hero "par excellence." His appearance on the Jewish scene is greeted with the derisive observation, "Can any good come from Nazareth?" (2) Where, indeed, could such a man develop such wisdom? "Is not his mother Mary, and his brothers James and Joseph?" (7) Who, in effect, is this peasant trying to kid? Even his choice of friends was comic relief: doubters, deniers, men with the smell of fish on their hands, prostitutes, tax collectors. He was a man, Isaiah had said, who would have no form, no comeliness, no beauty that we should desire him. (13) And so they mocked him, we are told, and blindfolded him, and played games with him, and dared him to guess, " . . . who is it that struck you." (5) And the sequence of comic events, beginning with his birth in a cave, culminated in the final absurdity that the man who claimed to be the King of kings ended his life impaled to a cross.

To make matters even more absurd, he also said such genuinely comical things. His sayings are just as quixotic as his deeds. "Unless you be as little children . . . " (8) "Unless a man lose his soul, he shall not find it." (6) "Unless you eat my flesh and drink my blood . . . " (3) He asked us to accept the perfectly ridiculous as the basis of morality: "Blessed are the meek, for they shall possess the earth." (9) And he topped off the series of mad aphorisms with the ultimate joke, "Before Abraham was, I am." (4)

Nor was all this simply unconscious with this clown. Laughter often was his weapon against the establishment. He observed that the priests and the lawyers were also adulterers in their hearts. His strategy of laughter was generally directed against those who presumed that they could resolve profound problems of life and death, good and evil by recourse to rules and regulations. The Divine cannot but laugh at pretentiousness.

Among the comic moments in the New Testament, the story of the daughter of Jairus looms large. (10) Jesus has been called to minister to Jairus' daughter, recently deceased. His first remark upon arrival is comic, ridiculous: "Why do you make so much noise and weep so? The child is not dead; she is asleep." The crowd is understandably incredulous. Anyone can observe that the girl is in fact dead, not asleep. And so, " . . . they laughed him to scorn." Here was a man who refused to accept the obvious, that death was the last word. But he put them all outside, and moments later, the girl emerged alive. As if to say "He who laughs last laughs best," the narrative ends abruptly with the laconic observation that " . . . they were overcome with amazement." The similarities between this narrative and the story of Abraham and Sarah, and a later incident in which the deceased Lazarus is the principal figure, are clear.

The fool, the clown can also be the seer, the prophet, because the madness of the fool can be an oracle. The fool is often the truly wise man, whether he cry as a voice in the wilderness, or as an imbecile prince, or a godly dolt, like the *jongleur de Notre Dame,* or as a poetic seer, like Arthur Rimbaud. And as Steppenwolf, he writes a diary of sorts for us, perceiving it to be "for madmen only," hoping that he (and we) will someday learn how to laugh. (21) At times, his intuition bears a touch of magic, as Lear's fool, who recognizes the folly of playing games in a world rent by tempest—and Lear's fool is certainly a "man for our times." He is often, as Jesus, a revolutionary simpleton. Apropos of the religious revolution, Kierkegaard insistently claimed that in order to be religious, a man must first of all be a comedian. (26)

We have a growing body of literature that attempts to describe the experience of this "higher madness," (22) which in our scientific moments we label insanity. No one speaks more graphically of the wisdom of the fool and the folly of the "wise man" than Ronald Laing:

Our sanity is not "true" sanity. Their madness is not "true" madness. The

madness of our patients is an artifact of the destruction wreaked on them by us and by them on themselves. Let no one suppose that we meet "true"
madness any more than that we are truly sane. The
madness that we encounter in "patients" is a gross
travesty, a mockery, a grotesque caricature of what
the natural healing of that estranged integration we
call sanity might be. (23)

"That same laughter, Madam,
is an irrelevancy which almost amounts to revelation," writes
Christopher Fry. (16) And it is this comic combination of the
irrelevant and revelation, the clownish and the prophetic that
is at the very root of the Christian tradition, whether we offi-
cially recognize it or not. Granted the Christian assumption
that Jesus is a God-man, he must then be the very epitome of
the incongruous, the figure of contradiction, the *perfect
clown.* So comic is this crazy mixture of the divine and the
human, the prophetic and the mad, the solemn and the ridiculous that Christian theologians have spent two thousand
agonizing years trying to explain the joke. And our cumula-
tive experience assures us again that the joke gets lost when
we try to explain it.

Jesus is a wedding of opposites.
Historically, we have been compelled by our tragic rational-
ism to find either/or solutions to explain him, or explain him
away. He becomes either God or man, but not both. The first
councils of the Church were all devoted in one way or another
to attempts to explain how Jesus could be God and man at the
same time. We ran through the Nestorian, the Monophysite,
the Arian and Semi-Arian solutions; and as attempts to explain
the mystery wore on into semantic hair-splitting, the simple
reality got lost, at least to theologians. A dear Jewish friend
once remarked to me, apropos of our rationalistic dualism,

that while the Jews could never accept the divinity of Jesus, Christians by and large have never quite been able to accept his humanity. We have been so busy trying to establish that he was God that we lost sight of the pleasantly comic fact that he was also palpably human. I think we could allow ourselves no more reverential meditation on the life of Jesus than to ponder the simple facts that he did, after all, get his feet dirty, pick his nose, and endure an occasional bowel movement. Ironically, it is precisely this central revelation that Christians have found so difficult to accept. Because Christians have been unwilling to laugh with God, we have been left a tragic, though ancient and venerable, dualistic tradition, stretching back to the Manichaeans, and touching us now through the twin forms of Protestant puritanism and Catholic Jansenism. It is because of this heritage that we tend to separate the divine from the human, the spiritual from the material, the soul from the body, the psyche from the soma, etc. And when we split man this way, we come inevitably to despise one of the poles: the human, the material, the body, the soma. We know this same effect in other languages as well. In medicine and psychology we have been the inheritors of the Cartesian split of the mind-body unit. In theology we are witnesses to the dissolution of religious integrity by a dualistic secularism that allows a man to split off his "religious" activities from his life, so classically described in Aldous Huxley's *Grey Eminence*. It is from this tragic dualistic tradition that we may now be just escaping. For it is the essence of tragedy to separate, to dichotomize; and it is the essence of comedy to accept what appears to be irreconcilable. Jesus is the archclown, because he is incongruity personified.

The clown also provokes laughter in us because he is essentially no one. He is at the same time many and none. His comic mask disguises true identity. In Jesus we have a perfect case of mistaken identity, or perhaps, in our vocabulary, a classic case of an identity crisis. Who is he? At the climax of his life, not even his closest friends recognize him. He is an unknown gardener to Mary Magdalen, an unrecognized fellow traveler to his own disciples, walking disconsolate from his execution, and a wandering fisherman to his apostles. The clown is no man and every man.

He is also often the victor, glancing cockily over his shoulder while sliding on the banana peel. He laughs at his own and others' pretensions. Hamlet's pretentious dilemma, "To be or not to be," is properly answered by the clown's ambivalence about how to peel the banana. The clown laughs, and makes us laugh, because he is laughing at our collective humanity, which he takes on himself as the scapegoat for unaccepted humanity. Again, Jesus is the clown-scapegoat; and his is the victory. The clown who dies in a painted mask of laughter, as most spectacularly painted by Rouault, is both terrible and funny. Rouault wrote this himself: "I see clearly that the clown is myself, ourselves, all of us. We are all clowns more or less. We all wear a spangled costume." (15) The clown is the God-in-us, and comedy is his way of keeping us honest. Sypher again comments:

> Strange to think, the death and rebirth of the god belong more fittingly to the comic than to the tragic theatre. Is this the reason why it is difficult for tragic art to deal with themes like the crucifixion and resurrection? Should we say that the drama of struggle, death and rebirth—Gethsemane, Calvary and Easter—actually belong in the comic rather than the tragic domain? The figure of Christ as god-man is surely the archetypal hero-victim. He is mocked, reviled, crowned with thorns—a comic scapegoat king. (27)

The meeting of death and life, the death-rebirth cycle, so familiar to psychoanalysis is essentially a comic opera.

To laugh is therefore to be unwilling to accept what is pretentious, disintegrated, dishonest, phony. The clown, the God-smiling-in-us, makes us smile at our own pretensions. Whoever pretends to be angelic or godlike is laughable; and whoever pretends to be an animal is laughable. The pompous clergyman who slips and falls on his flowing vestments is a mere man. And so a slip of the tongue is funnier coming from the mouth of the pulpit orator, as in the classic story of preacher who announced from his pulpit that those ladies in the congregation who wished to become members of the mothers' club should meet him in his office after the service. So also the man who poses as a horse or a goat is really only Uncle Fred. It is the God laughing in us that makes it impossible for us to accept either our divine or our animal pretensions. And the God laughing in us was incarnate in the person of Jesus.

His laughter must ripple now at the pretensions of official churchmen, declaring saints to be or not to be in solemn pronouncement, daring to dispel his mystery with rules and regulations, and explaining away his infinite joke with written formulas. We have forgotten Kierkegaard, and his caution that humor is at the heart of the truly religious experience. One's relationship with God is far too important to be taken seriously. When we do that, our vision gets quickly translated into structures and organizations, and with them come the rituals and games that one is obliged to play. The games are there as a substitute for the original experience. Perhaps the pretension of the churchman is matched only by that of those dissidents who attack the game with the same earnest frenzy with which it is defended. We appear to need to take the game seriously, regardless of whether that be done with the intent of defending the game or of doing battle with it. The clown, on the other hand, focuses on the absurdity of both ventures with a comic gesture that leaves us with the sole alternative of accepting ourselves for precisely what we are.

The role of laughter, and the laughter of the gods, is therefore directed to one objective, the putting together of what seems to be irreconcilable. Laughter acknowledges the coexistence of the divine and the human, of joy and sorrow, of laughter and tears. The truly absurd fact is that the pathetic itself is inherent in the comic. So it is that one is tempted both to laugh and to weep when the humorist speaks. The union of opposites, the incongruous is the playground of the clown. And that role is most clearly manifest in the presence of the God-in-us, the Christ.

Kahlil Gibran, who loved paradoxes and who was himself a figure of contradiction, the mad-wise man, in his own life, says it well:

Your joy is sorrow unmasked.
And the selfsame well from which your laughter
rises was often time filled with your tears.
And how else can it be?
The deeper that sorrow carves into your being, the
more joy you can contain. (17)

Putting together and accepting the union of what seems to be opposed: that was the work of Jesus. It is also the mystery of psychotherapy. It need scarcely be observed that putting together what seems opposed is a dialectic process. And at the very end of that comic rainbow, there one finds the clown, the omega, the Nirvana, the God. It all depends, as that most perfect clown Quixote would remind us, on where one looks to find Him. We have, historically, searched for God on the mountaintop, the holy place of the ancients, as Robinson describes. (24) Finding Him unapproachable there, we found Him in others, led by the New Testament directive that He would be among the least of His little ones. But that pursuit is not without its own deceptions. And so, ultimately, we search through that place where he may always have been, within ourselves, where the image of God lurks. And there, the God-within-us, I should like to suggest, remains quite alive and smiling.

Bibliography

1. Bergson, Henri: Laughter. In, *Comedy*. New York: Doubleday–Anchor Books, 1956, p. 62.

2. John 1:46

3. John 6:54

4. John 8:58

5. Mark 14:65

6. Mark 8:35

7. Matt. 13:55

8. Matt. 18:3

9. Matt. 5:4

10. Matt. 9:18–19, 23–25

11. Gen. 17:16

12. Gen. 22:2

13. Isa. 53

14. Psa. 21

15. Courthion, Pierre: *Georges Rouault*. New York: Harry N. Abrams, 1961, p. 86.

16. Fry, Christopher: *The Lady's Not for Burning*. New York: Oxford University Press, 1950, p. 49.

17. Gibran, Kahlil: *The Prophet*. New York: Alfred A. Knopf, 1968, p. 29.

18. Grotjahn, Martin: *Beyond Laughter*. New York: McGraw-Hill, 1957, p. 7.

19. Grotjahn, *op. cit.*, p. 26.

20. Hesse, Hermann: *Steppenwolf*. New York: Holt, Rinehart, and Winston, Rinehart Edition, 1963, p. 4.

21. Hesse, *op. cit.*, pp. 25,218.

22. Kaplan, Bert (Ed.): *The Inner World of Mental Illness*. New York: Harper & Row, 1964.

23. Laing, Ronald D., *The Politics of Experience*. New York: Pantheon, 1967, p. 101.

24. Robinson, John A. T.: *Honest to God*. Philadelphia: Westminster Press, 1963.

25. Sypher, Wylie: The meanings of comedy. In: *Comedy*. New York: Doubleday–Anchor Books, 1956, p. 237.

26. Sypher, *op. cit.*, p. 234.

27. Sypher, *op. cit.*, p. 220.

28. Watts, Alan W.: *Psychotherapy, East and West*. New York: Ballantine Books, 1961, pp. 64ff.

13/

Jewish Jokes and Their Relation to Masochism

Martin Grotjahn, M.D.

> *Unextinguished laughter*
> *of the gods shakes the skies.*

The Gentile should step gingerly when talking about the Jewish joke. The Jewish population is so sensitive at the present time and so sensitized to anti-Semitism, that only a Jew is allowed to discuss the problems involved in being Jewish. A Gentile wishing to be heard is easily suspected even if he only recognizes the presence of the Jewish question. Often in my life I have identified myself with my Jewish friends, and I joined them in their exodus from Germany. I have been diagnosed as an "honorary Jew."

We laugh when the joke gives us an occasion for guilt-free expression of aggression. In a joke or a witticism, aggression is activated, carefully disguised so that we do not feel guilty about it. This frees us from repression, and this energy which is no longer needed for repression is turned to laughter, as Freud has described it. The Jewish joke has a special place among witticisms. Like every joke, it is a guilt-free expression of aggression, but this aggression is directed against the Jewish person himself. It is aggression turned inward. It is a combination of a sadistic attack with masochistic indulgence.

In order to see the difference between the ordinary joke and the special features of the Jewish joke, we may, at first, study the peculiar fact that there is very little laughter in the Bible. The necessity for irreverence, which is essential for the dynamics of laughter, is incompatible with the spirit of the Judeo-Christian tradition. In that respect, the Bible is unlike the *Iliad* or the *Odyssey,* where we hear the "unextinguished laughter of the gods shakes the skies."

Sarah, the wife of Abraham, is perhaps the only person in the Bible who laughs. When the Angel of the Lord announced that she would bear a child to Abraham, "Sarah laughed." Later Sarah denied she laughed and said, "I laugh not," for she was afraid. And He said, "Nay, but thou didst laugh." When the child was born, Abraham was over one hundred years old. Sarah named the child Isaac, which means "the laughing one," because he was conceived in his parents' old age. And Sarah said, "God hath made me to laugh so that all that hear will laugh with me." (Genesis 21:6)

It is possible that a reference to laughter has been lost in the Bible. In the book of Genesis (9: 18–26) Noah, being the first husbandman, planted a vineyard, drank from his wine and became drunk. While he was lying uncovered in his tent, Ham, the father of Canaan, saw the nakedness of his father. In the usual translations (King James and the Revised Standard Version) the sentence continues, "and told his two brothers." The original text implies that the proper translation may be "and laughingly told his two brothers." After they heard what Ham told them, his two brothers took a garment, laid it upon their shoulders and went backward to cover their father so that they would not see his nakedness. When Noah awoke from his stupor he "knew what his younger son had done unto him. And he said, 'Cursed be Canaan; a servant of servants shall he be unto his brethren.'"

In Jewish folklore, and also in the Babylonian Talmud commentaries, it is implied that Ham did more to Noah than simply look at him—that he may have castrated him, and then triumphantly told his brothers what he had done. This version of the story about Noah and his sons contains the original conflict which in disguised form is the motif from which comedy developed as a new form of art in later stages of history. (The reversed Oedipus, the casting of the father in the role of the castrated son.)

According to Sigmund Freud and Theodor Reik, no other people on earth, in the past or the present time, has taken itself so mercilessly as the butt of its own jokes as the Jewish people. It is as if the Jewish joke in sophisticated refinement shows the cruel enemy how to be hostile and still remain human. The Jewish joke, however, is only a masochistic mask; it is by no means a sign of masochistic perversion. The Jewish joke constitutes victory by defeat. The persecuted Jew who makes himself the butt of the joke deflects his dangerous hostility away from the persecutors onto himself. The result is not defeat or surrender, but victory and greatness.

While listening to the Jewish joke, one can almost see how a witty Jewish man carefully and cautiously takes a sharp dagger out of his enemy's hands, sharpens it so that it can split a hair in midair, polishes it until it shines brightly, stabs himself with it, then returns it gallantly to the anti-Semite with the silent reproach: Now see whether you can do it half as well. Here is one such story:

A number of Jews were debating whose synagogue was the most progressive one. One man said that in his temple they kept an ashtray near the Torah so that even the reader could continue to smoke.

The second man claimed, "We are much more progressive. At Yom Kippur we serve sandwiches—ham sandwiches, that is."

While everybody was considering this piece of progress, a third man ended all further competition with his statement, "We are so progressive, that we have a neon sign on top of our temple: Closed because of Holy Days."

With one sweeping statement, he neatly finished Judaism.

The Jewish joke seems to be directed against the self, or the enlarged self as represented by one's own people. Weakness is shown with obvious enjoyment and a feeling of liberation and relief: Look who is laughing!

In all these jokes there is no promise to change the offending situation or to meet the demands of the enemy. All contain a kind of melancholy resignation and occasionally a stubborn pledge: This is the way we are and will be as long as we are Jewish.

Aggression turned against the self seems to be an essential feature of the truly Jewish joke. It is as if the Jew tells his enemies: You do not need to attack us. We can do that ourselves—and even better. We can take it, and we will come out all right. We know our weakness and, in a way, we are proud of it.

To the sharpness of Jewish wit, the greatness and kindness of humor is added in a rare combination:

A little Jew came running to his rabbi, crying, "Rabbi, a terrible thing has happened. My son wants to marry a Gentile girl!"

"Your son!" said the rabbi, "Look at me and my son. Here am I, the leader of the community. Everyone looks up to me as an example, and looks up to my family; and my son wants to marry a Gentile girl and wants to be baptized."

After a silence, the little Jew said, "Everyone comes to you with their problems, but what do you do when you have such a terrible problem? To whom do you turn?"

"What can I do? I turned to God."

"And? What did God tell you?"

God said to me, "Your son! . . . Look at mine."

Another example symbolizes in highly condensed form the eternal, unanalyzable conflict of an only son of a Jewish mother:

A mother gave her son two neckties as a present. The son wants to show his appreciation and wears one. Says the mother, "What's the matter? Don't you like the other one?"

What happened here? The aggressive thought "Mothers are no good. Mothers are tricky. Mothers turn things around. A son never wins," is repressed, disguised, and then admitted to consciousness. Repressive energy is freed and is released in laughter. The masochistic element becomes visible in the thought, "Mothers want to suffer. They turn things against themselves, no matter how. A son does not need to feel guilty about that."

One other joke illustrates another aspect of a minority group:

A lady asked the driver of her bus, "Are you Jewish?" He said, "No."

After a while the lady asks again.

With slight irritation, the bus driver answers again, "No, I am not Jewish."

The lady does not give up. She can't let go of her question.

Finally, trying to finish this topic, the bus driver says, "Okay, lady, have it your way. I am Jewish." With an expression of deep satisfaction, the lady leans back, has one more good look at him and says, "You don't look it!"

The aggressive thought in this joke is the lady's intention to claim the bus driver as a member of her minority group, and when he reluctantly accepts the honor, to deny it to him. It is an ambivalent play with the privilege, the curse, the honor, and the right to call oneself Jewish.

An old and venerable Jew felt that his time had run out and that he would die in a few days. He called his three best friends: a schoolteacher, a minister, and his rabbi. He distributed all he owned—a cash fortune of $90,000—and asked each of his friends, as a last favor, to throw $30,000 into his grave so that it could be buried with him.

Within two days the old man died, and he was buried. Later the three friends meet, and after some embarrassed silence, the teacher confesses that he has kept $10,000, and has thrown into the open grave only $20,000. He needed the money to start a library for underprivileged children in his school. After more silence, the minister confesses that he has kept $15,000 and that the Lord will forgive him, because he has used the money for a badly needed Sunday school, which will now carry on the memory of the deceased one.

Knowing what was expected of him, the rabbi waited a moment, and then stated kindly and with good conscience, "The Lord does not need to forgive me anything; I buried with our friend a check for the whole amount."

The wit is related to sadism and to aggression. Humor is related to masochism and suffering. The Jewish joke stands in between.

There is not a Jewish unconscious, as there is not a Jewish brain or a Jewish cancer. In the strictest sense of the word, there also is not a Jewish character type. There are perhaps certain trends in the Jewish person which develop as his specific way of adjustment to his environment, his idea of being Jewish, his tradition and identity. There is something we call "Jewish wit," which is significant for an adjustment of the Jewish personality, and born out of the needs of his unconscious, trained by his early infantile upbringing, and grown in response to his environment.

There are some specific features in the Jewish education, the Jewish background and environment, which may perhaps help to explain some character trends which we often assign to the Jewish person. For instance, the Jewish mother seems to expect to have borne in her son a Messiah and she loves him fiercely. Whoever has

141

been born as an only son of a Jewish mother will know what that means—consciously and unconsciously.

Born as a potential Messiah, the Jewish boy lives to recognize that the Gentiles do not see in him exactly that—but just a Jew, a member of a minority. He is born to become a Messiah; he lives to see that he is a hated enemy. It is a tough adjustment to make—that switch from the expectation of a mother to the recognition of reality.

The Jewish mother is different from the Spartanic mother, who expects her son to be a hero, no matter whether he is dead or alive. The Jewish mother hopes for victory, but accepts defeat—in a way, almost expects it. The masochistic adjustment aims at victory by defeat.

The Jewish mother tells her son, "Be careful. Never listen to the goy. Swallow insults. Keep the law. Be patient. You are one of God's chosen people and precious in His sight. One day, He will make us a nation again." This is difficult for the sensitive Gentile to understand. A Gentile may feel inferior and guilty because he has not suffered a million slights and snubs and insults, and he still will identify with Jesus who suffered so much (Theodor Reik).

The secret of the Jewish masochism is anchored in the holy words, "The meek shall inherit the world." For having told us that we, the Gentiles, blame the Jews, we were happy to kill our enemies and even to eat them; and now we are supposed to love them. As it is written in Leviticus, "You shall love your neighbor as yourself." This is a tough assignment, and it implies a heavy burden put on our conscious and unconcious hostility. For the Jewish person, the task of loving one's neighbor is exacting enough to discourage all other mystical speculation about the nature of God. The Jewish religion is essentially a practical religion, a guide to the conduct of daily life.

To the Gentile's regret, Jesus was a descendant of David, and not of King Alfred. Jesus was a king of the Jews, and not the king of any other people. We, the Christians, believe in the Son of Man, but he was born to God's chosen people who do not recognize him. We believe that we are the "right believers," but the Jewish people are, and remain, His chosen people. To the Jews, and not to the Gentiles, were committed the holy oracles of God. This is why Christians feel so often as if we were the lost tribes of Israel.

Not much insight into human behavior is gained when the ethical demand for equality of men is taken as a scientific fact. Equally little is gained if presumed or factual differences between people are evaluated to establish a value system of superiority and inferiority, often related to majority and minority groups.

I have tried here, with the example of something commonly called "The Jewish Joke," to analyze some differences in the character of jokes, perhaps leading back to character traits which can be explained through specific factors in the early infantile mother-child relationship, through tradition and ideology, all reflected in the individual and generic unconscious.

Such analysis should lead to better communication and interaction on conscious and unconscious levels. This may help to build a basis of acceptance, tolerance, and integration between people, so desperately needed at a time when technology outdistanced human maturation.

It is this hope which analytic psychology has to offer for the future.

Annotated Bibliography

Some of my thoughts have been expressed in my book, *Beyond Laughter* (New York: McGraw–Hill, 1957). There proper reference is given to Sigmund Freud's book on jokes, wit, and humor, and to Theodor Reik's book on masochism. (*Masochism in Modern Man.* New York: Farrar, Straus & Co., 1941, and See *Jewish Wit,* New York: The Gamut Press, 1962), also my paper: "On Bullfighting and the Future of Tragedy" (*Int. J. Psychoanal.,* 40:238–239, 1959), and a paper to be published on "Martin Luther, Sigmund Freud, and Albert Schweitzer," a contribution to Albert Schweitzer's 85th birthday.

Robert Graves published an excellent article "What It Feels Like to Be a Goy" (*Commentary,* 27:413–419, 1959).

In many ways my thoughts, as expressed in this paper, are reactions and commentaries to the work of Sidney Tarachow, for instance, his classic paper: "Remarks on the Comic Process and Beauty" (*Psychoanal. Quart.,* 18:215–226, 1949), and his outstanding paper on "Circuses and Clowns" (in *Psychoanalysis and the Social Sciences,* 3:171–188; New York: Int. Univ. Press, 1951). Finally and most recently Sidney Tarachow wrote, after having published his research on the Apostle Paul, a most thoughtful study: "Judas: The Beloved Executioner" (*Psychoanal. Quart.,* 29:528–554, 1960).

14/

"Black"/Black Humor: The Renaissance of Laughter

Joseph Boskin, Ph.D.

The happy resurgence of humor in many of its forms is an indication of a clearer perspective of the past and ability to confront the present.

Answering a direct query about the nature of humor, Charlie Chaplin remarked that "It is a kind of gentle and benevolent custodian which prevents us from being overwhelmed by the apparent seriousness of life." Unlike other opiates, humor achieves its therapeutic results from a confrontation with reality, not a denial of it. Thus, as both an individual and collective device, humor casts a penetrating light of revelation which may be harsh and unsettling.

The potential of humor to serve as a custodian of our national balance, however, has not always been utilized. In recent decades two distinct periods emerge in clear contrast to one another. In terms of national humor, the first of the two periods might easily be described as one of aridity. From the Korean War to the last years of Eisenhower's tenure in office, a sense of confusion coupled with anxiety stifled laughter in the land. Lamentations on the decline of American humor in the 1950s were heard from many quarters. Early in the decade Walt Kelly, the creator of "Pogo," called for the "crying need for the cleansing lash of laughter." Kenneth Rexroth, the noted commentator on the "beat" generation, wrote an angry article entitled "The Decline of American Humor," which was in itself ironic since the fiction of the "beats" was dull-panned and vacuous. Robert Hatch observed a similar malaise in the theater, commenting that "during the past ten to fifteen years it has become increasingly hazardous to laugh in the theater." And at the close of the decade, with his head half turned in derision, historian Eric Goldman capped these feelings of anguish in an essay with the epitaph: "Goodbye to the fifties—and good riddance."

By the end of the 1950s, however, conditions had changed enough to produce a certain amount of whimsy and wit. With the lessening of international and domestic tensions, the election in 1960 of a president endowed with a sophisticated wit, the rise of a new generation of humorists and satirists who equaled in intensity and pungency their counterparts of the 1920s to the 1940s, and more importantly, the emergence of Afro-American humor, there has been a revival of American laughter. This happy resurgence of humor in many of its forms—wit, satire, mimicry, serio-comedy—is an indication of a clearer perspective of the past and an ability to confront the present. Subjects once considered off-limits—politics, presidents, foreign policy, even certain forms of ethnic behavior—are subjects probed by the new humorists in all of the mass media. We are, then, in a period which might be described as a midcentury renaissance of laughter. It is a welcome relief from the banality of the previous decade.

However refreshing, one direction of contemporary humor has been subjected to severe criticism. "To the unquestioning audience," a *Time* magazine editorial lamented,

> the state of American comedy may appear to be healthy indeed. The proliferation of comedy into every corner of American life, the spreading hipness and general joking seem to indicate one of the richest times for comedy in American history. But do they? (1)

Time was concerned for the future of American humor. "A closer examination of current comedy reveals neither a renaissance nor reformation but the beginnings of what could, unless it is reversed, become the dark-ages of American humor." (1) Two developments in particular have been noted as contributing to this undermining of comedy: the lack of restraint in humorous analysis and the emergence of "black humor."

The unflinching iconoclasm of humorous analysis, the spoofing of all areas of existence including death and destruction, has been particularly disturbing. The argument posed by detractors is that with the lack of conscious limitations the slender line between seriousness and comedy is dulled if not destroyed. The consequence of this fusion is the hardening of sensibilities, the inability to distinguish between humor which presents a necessary perspective, and responsibility which depends upon a quiet rationality.

"Black humor" is inextricably related to a particular literary development. Bruce Jay Friedman has suggested that the style of fiction related to "black humor" has its roots in the "chord of absurdity" struck by merely recording the events of the present age. "What has occurred," Friedman suggests, is that the satirist has had his ground usurped by the newspaper reporter. The journalist, who in the year 1964, must cover the ecumenical debate of whether Jews on the one hand, are still to be known as Christ-killers, or, on the other are to be let off the hook, is certainly today's satirist. The novelist-satirist, with no real territory of his own to roam, has had to discover new land, invent a new currency, a new set of filters, has had to sail into darker waters somewhere beyond satire and I think this is what is meant by black humor. (2)

Beyond the practical consideration of literary expediency, however, is the fact that to many writers existence does indeed appear to be on an absurd level. The fiction of "black humor" is an indication that the behavior of the world is its own exaggeration; thus the need for humorous distortion is minimized.

Whatever its origins, the humor of the absurd has been alternately castigated and defended. Denigrators have argued that this type of humor does not make people laugh; rather they say that it deals with serious subjects in a macabre fashion. Conversely, Leslie Fiedler has contended that "black humor" is the only valid posture that contemporary work can adopt. Thus, both the sacrilegious nature of humor and its accent on the absurdity of man's behavior are combined in American society.

A second significant development in American humor in the 1960s was the rise to national prominence of Afro-American humor and humorists. The recognized stature of Godfrey Cambridge, Dick Gregory, "Moms" Mabley, Pigmeat Markham, Bill Cosby, Nipsey Russell, Richard Pryor, Flip Wilson and others reflects the growing acceptance of the Negro's insistent ethnic challenge to the social structure through a humor which is the mark of a group struggling fiercely to achieve a desired status.

Contemporary black humor—or, rather, the humor of the Afro-American as it is now being communicated to whites for the first time—has destroyed the stereotype of the Afro-American as a "Sambo." To the Caucasian the Negro has constantly been portrayed as lazy, shiftless, being capable of great acts of animal violence. On the basis of this conception, there was created a vast labyrinth of laws, social customs and folkways directed against bringing the black man into white culture. To perpetuate the image, it was essential to deny the African and his descendants a range of social and intellectual capacities, among them being the ability to translate life experiences into humor. One prejudice reinforced the other. By refusing to recognize the complexity and depth of Negro humor, society was able to maintain its caste system and its imbalance.

Thus, it is extremely important that the Afro-American folk tradition is only now finding access to white society after being blocked for centuries. It is not only a testimony to the central position which the black man occupies in contemporary American thought, but it is also an indication of the degree to which a confrontation contributes to the stability and balance of a pluralistic social order.

In a very real sense, black humor is certainly not "new." It is similar to, though not at all identical with, the structure or nature of other ethnic group humor. What can be said briefly is that due to the obscurity to which it has been relegated by prejudice and segregation, it is practically unknown to the majority of Caucasians. Even the sophisticated humorist Ogden Nash expressed astonishment about the reach of black humor. In his review of Langston Hughes' work, *The Book of Negro Humor,* Nash wrote:

The range of humor here collected is a surprise. One would not have expected so many kinds, from so many sources. There are the contemporary comics . . . There are jokes having to do with jive and the blues. There are anecdotes from the pulpit. There are stories from Orleans and Harlem. (3)

This surprise at the welter of primary material in existence is not altogether unwarranted. Prior to the Black Revolution of the Sixties, the humor of the Afro-American had been introduced essentially by whites. As might be expected, many of the resultant stories and anecdotes reflected the attitudes and values of the dominant culture. Blacks were seen as no more than caricatures, sources or objects of ridicule, well-intentioned inepts by most whites.

Segregation in almost all areas of American life, but particularly in the fields of entertainment and mass communication, further compounded the situation by blocking the emergence of humorists who could have corrected the picture. Afro-American storytellers and comedians in the past have played mainly to black audiences. Few persons outside the black community prior to the contemporary period could have identified such able Negro humorists as "Moms" Mabley, "Slapsey" White, Pigmeat Markham, Redd Foxx, George Kirby, Timmy Rogers and others.

A study of humor has certain limitations, not the least of these being E. B. White's admonition: "Humor can be dissected as a frog can, but the thing dies in the process and the innards are discouraging to any but the pure scientific mind." Other liabilities are perhaps equally obvious. Nevertheless, as one of the most important characteristics of human behavior, black laughter is essential to the national perspective and psyche.

150

Black humor in all its essential forms—serio-comedy, parody, mimicry, satire, exaggerations, buffoonery, wit, gallows humor—can be characterized as the humor of the outsider and the rejected. Two outstanding features of black humor were its defensive qualities, which were intended to ward off punishment and reflected a deep pathos, and an aggressive tendency which until recently was quietly desperate, tension releasing and relied heavily upon role-reversal for its source of retaliation. In the Fifties and Sixties the humor lost its defensive tone and became instead a powerful technique used in the creation of group cohesion and the denigration of the white establishment. Further, unlike the early humor under the slavery and caste systems, aggressive expressions were spoken openly to white audiences. In some instances—for example, the several television specials in the late Sixties which used Afro-American humor as their format—blacks attempted to convey the humorous side of life in the community. Thus black humor underwent changes of significant proportion in the period of militancy. Early black humor emanated from an African base and was quickly fused with survival objectives. A mythical sign at the edge of a Southern town from which Negroes were barred pointed up a warning:

If you can read this sign,

run

If you can't read this sign,

run anyway

To make his oppressor laugh and secure those items necessary for survival, slaves became adroit at turning situations around: The inability of blacks to protect themselves led to a large number of stories, many of which were in the "gallows humor" genre. Their indefensibility was noted in this anecdote:

As a Negro woman was riding on a bus, a louse suddenly began crawling up her back. A white woman noticed it and picked it off. The Negro turned to her and said sharply, "Put it back, put it back. Everything we Negroes get, you people try to take away from us."

More sharply "gallows" was the post-World War II story about a black soldier who met a French girl and married her:

The soldier decided to bring the girl of his dreams back to his home town in Mississippi and wrote to his U.S. Senator, Theodore Bilbo, of his plans. A few weeks later he received a reply from the Senator's office: "Have hung your letter in my office. Am waiting on you."

Perhaps the cruelest gibe indicating the previous state of tenuous existence of the black was contained in the old quip: "A black hen laid a white egg and they hung her." That the white world was overpowering in all areas whether real or imaginary was the basis of an old nursery story. "Mirror, mirror, on the wall," asked a Negro girl as she stood before the reflecting glass, "who is the fairest one of all?" "Snow White, you black bitch" answered the mirror "and don't you forget it."

Compensation from the malaise of position was accomplished by either "fooling master" or by devising humorous histories which reversed the traditional roles of inferior/superior. There is a vast lexicon of anecdotes related by ex-slaves in the voluminous Slave Narratives. One of the most telling involved a group of hungry slaves who developed an ingenious scheme for securing choice meats for themselves. The story is important not only for its insight into survival techniques but primarily because it was subsequently used by generations of blacks to highlight a victory over the foolish white:

. . . . I remember Mammy told me about one master who almost starved his slaves. Mighty stingy, I reckon he was.

Some of them slaves was so poorly thin they ribs would kinda rustle against each other like corn stalks a-drying in the hot winds. But they gets even one hog-killing time, and it was funny, too, Mammy said.

They was seven hogs, fat and ready for fall hog-killing time. Just the day before Old Master told off they was to be killed, something happened to all them porkers. One of the field boys found them and come a-telling the master: "The hogs is all died, now they won't be any meats for the winter."

When the master gets to where at the hogs is laying, they's a lot of Negroes standing round looking sorrow-eyed at the wasted meat. The master asks: "What's the illness with 'em?"

"Malitis," they tells him, and they acts like they don't want to touch the hogs. Master says to dress them anyway for they ain't no more meat on the place.

He says to keep all the meat for the slave families, but that's because he's afraid to eat it hisself account of the hogs' got malitis.

"Don't you all know what is malitis?" Mammy would ask the children when she was telling of the seven fat hogs and seventy lean slaves. And she would laugh, remembering how they fooled Old Master so's to get all them good meats.

"One of the strongest Negroes got up early in the morning," Mammy would explain, "long 'fore the rising horn called the slaves from their cabins. He skitted to the hog pen with a heavy mallet in his hand. When he tapped Mister Hog 'tween the eyes with that mallet, 'malitis' set in mighty quick, but is was a uncommon 'disease,' even with hungry Negroes around all the time."

Inversion—the process of reversing the role of inferior and superior—was a technique blacks often used to overcome the stupidity of prejudice. On the subject of stealing to which blacks are supposedly addicted:

A white minister arrived in Africa and was met by an African chief and his party. The chief indicated to the minister that his bags would be picked up by his men and transported to the interior. But first he wanted to show him around the village. The minister demurred, pointing to his belongings. The chief allayed his fears: "You don't have to worry about your bags," he said, "there isn't a white man within a hundred miles of here."

On the subject of white intelligence, this comparison:

A colored maid and her white employer became pregnant at the same time and gave birth on the same day. A few months later the white woman came running into the kitchen and exclaimed to the maid: "My baby said his first word today!" In the crib the colored baby sat up and said, "He did? He did? What did he say?"

The theme that whites would some day be held accountable for the sins perpetuated against nonwhites served as the basis of several stories. Intriguingly, the place of the jokes was in the afterworld, indicating the degree to which the black man was blocked in expressing his aggressiveness. An illustration is the conversation between two racist governors of Georgia, Gene Talmadge and his son Herman:

> Georgia's Governor Herman (Hummon) Talmadge called in a spiritualist to contact his pappy, the late Governor, "Old Gene" Talmadge. "Pappy," asked Hummon, "How mah doin' up here?" "All right, son," replied Old Gene, "But, son, go easy on that white primary bill. They got a nigger fireman down here."

Thus the humor of the Afro-American prior to the militant decades of the fifties and sixties reflected the position of the "enslaved": one who, in a lowly status and unable to protect himself, devised the humor of survival and of passive-aggressive. With the onslaught of the Civil Rights movement, however, black attitudes and expressions began to quickly change—although within the context of changes several features remained essentially in operative fashion. Whites, for example, were still portrayed as uncivilized and many stories about their brutality were circulated by civil rights workers. One macabre joke has as its setting the Gates of Heaven:

> One day a young black showed up at the Pearly Gates and was met by St. Peter. "I would like to be admitted into Heaven, St.

Peter" said the black. "Fine, fine, but tell me what you have done lately which would permit you to be admitted?"

"Well," answered the man, "I marched from Selma to Montgomery, Alabama in a civil rights march."

"Umm. You know, lots of people marched from Selma to Montgomery," replied St. Peter. "Have you done anything else?"

"Yes, I got married on the Court House steps in Montgomery, Alabama at noon."

"What's so unusual about that?" asked St. Peter.

"I married a white woman."

St. Peter's eyes opened wide. "You married a white woman on the Court House steps in Montgomery, Alabama at twelve o'clock noon!? When was that?"

"Oh," answered the man, "about two minutes ago."

Of themselves, however, the Afro-Americans exulted in a sense of mission and accomplishment which came through in barbs, quips and mocking laughter. Dr. Martin Luther King summed up the change in a speech at a Civil Rights rally in 1964 with an old slave witticism: "We ain't what we ought to be and we ain't what we want to be and we ain't what we're going to be. But thank God, we ain't what we was."

Open challenge and chiding admonishment thus became major elements in black humor. Leroi Jones and a friend mocked the stereotypes by eating a watermelon with several others on a busy Washington, D.C.

thoroughfare; black workers refused to clean Ku Klux Klan robes in North Carolina; students in a Chicago high school refused to march in graduation excercises because the music for the process was from the opera *Aida* in which the central figure is a slave; Dick Gregory playfully threatened to picket the U.S. Weather Bureau until they named a hurricane after Beulah; college students carried on sensitivity sessions wearing white masks. Multiplied across the country, these expressions echoed as a chorus of militancy in humor.

Triumph over whites was heard in many different stories in the period. One joke focused on two aspects of prejudice: one an example of institutionalized racism, the other an example of black cleverness:

Two pilots, one white and one black, were at the controls of an airplane. Suddenly the plane developed engine trouble and it became clear that it was going to crash. The white pilot shouted to his co-pilot: "Well, I finally found a way to get rid of you. I never wanted you to be my co-pilot so I hid one parachute aboard." From the distance came a voice: "I know, I know."

In addition to the sense of power over events, the humor of militancy reflected a high degree of self-acceptance. It can be argued that the highest form of laughter involves the ability to laugh at oneself, to mock the features ascribed to by others. Several interesting stories circulated during the sixties not only knocked prejudice but twisted the situation in such a way that the rationale for its basis appeared ludicrous. A black man is engaged in a dialogue with God:

Tell me, Lord, how come I'm so black?

157

YOU'RE BLACK SO THAT YOU COULD WITHSTAND THE HOT RAYS OF THE SUN.

Tell me, Lord, how come my hair is so nappy?

YOUR HAIR IS NAPPY SO THAT YOU WOULD NOT SWEAT PROFUSELY UNDER THE HOT RAYS OF THE SUN.

Tell me, Lord, how come my legs are so long?

YOUR LEGS ARE LONG SO THAT YOU COULD ESCAPE FROM THE WILD BEASTS IN THE HOT SUN OF AFRICA.

Tell me, Lord, what the hell am I doing in Chicago?

Thus, the humor of the Afro-American has come a considerable distance from its secrecy and defensiveness to one of open hostility and aggressiveness. But the most important change is to be found in its reflection of group awareness and acceptance. In this blacks share the foibles of other groups as described by Walt Kelly's "Pogo." Pogo and his friends spent the better part of a day seeking their enemy. Finally tired, they sat down in the swamp. Pogo looked around and exclaimed: "Friends, we have met the enemy and they is Us." The liberation of American culture from its racial hangup begins with that statement.

Bibliography:

1. American Humor: Hardly a Laughing Matter. *Time,* LXXXVII, March 4, 1966, p. 46.

2. Friedman, Bruce Jay: *Black Humor.* New York: Bantam Books, 1965, p. ix.

3. Nash, Ogden: Book Review on: Hughes, Langston: *The Book of Negro Humor. Los Angeles Times Calendar,* March 13, 1966, p. 33.

15/

Laughter and Sex

Martin Grotjahn, M.D.

*Mature enjoyment of sex
should be free, easy, graceful, and spontaneous.*

Sex is no laughing matter, and badly timed laughter or even a giggle may turn out to be the perfect squelch during intercourse. If one considered laughter during sex relations, one could only advise, "Don't!" A popular magazine recently published a letter from a startled young man who was stricken impotent by his bride who broke into uncontrollable peals of laughter when she saw her young husband react to her with an erection. Such laughter, of course, is a reaction to anxiety and requires psychiatric help.

Many a tourist from Europe or America visiting in Japan has been quite unnerved by the giggles of the girls, which are the traditional expression of their approval for their guests. Japanese girls had to be restrained not to giggle for the gentlemen of the Western culture, and to reserve their giggles for Orientals.

On the other hand it would be terrible to take sex as a deadly serious matter. Mature enjoyment of sex should be free, easy, graceful, and spontaneous;

161

such ease should not exclude sexually stimulating laughter.

Much has been written about the psychology of jokes, but it was Sigmund Freud who offered the first insight into the unconscious dynamics of laughter and wit. He wrote his famous book *Jokes and Their Relation to the Unconscious* (1) as a companion volume to his *Dream Interpretation* (2) and published it in 1905. It is the first dynamic explanation of the psychology of laughter as it is also the first insight into creativity, artistic and otherwise.

According to Freud, laughter occurs when psychic energy is stimulated, then temporarily repressed, and finally freely and suddenly released without guilt or conflict. This sometimes happens, for example, when aggressive energy is freed from repression; the more energy that is suddenly expressed, the louder and deeper the laughter will sound. A direct, undisguised outlet of aggression is not funny and an act of violence does not lead to laughter. An aggressive intent must be stimulated, then repressed from consciousness into the unconscious; there it must be carefully disguised by the work of unconscious censorship and finally allowed to emerge again—now in the disguise of a joke which expresses the hostile aggressive intent successfully. Freud compared this work of disguise in the unconscious with a train entering, passing, and then emerging again out of a mountain tunnel. In the darkness an aggressive trend has been disguised as a joke and is now allowed to be experienced harmlessly. The dream symbolizes and fulfills symbolically a wish; wit expresses an aggressive trend in disguise.

The joke is judged according to the eloquence of the disguise. The wit work is completed when the aggressive or hostile trend remains recognizable, but is so disguised that we can allow it to be expressed freely. The person who conceives the witty remark or the joke feels

162

compelled to tell it to a second person in order to test the disguise. The laughter of the person who listens to the joke thus reveals that aggressive trends in him have been stimulated and that he too recognizes the hostility in the joke, appreciates the witty disguise, and he has also released aggression from repression.

One more important dynamic function is needed in a good joke—the release of aggression disguised in acceptable form must be sudden and must be combined with some infantile pleasure, as for instance, voyeurism, exhibitionism, sadism, play with words, or double meaning.

To understand this let us compare the direct expression of aggression, such as hitting a man with a hammer, which is not funny at all, with the slapstick humor of hitting someone in the face with a pie. This vents aggression rather harmlessly but is not good humor because the aggression is not well disguised. Compare it, for example, with the story of the man brought before the judge for bootlegging. The judge tells the defendant that, even though they didn't catch him actually making moonshine, he must consider him guilty because there was a still and moonshine on his premises. To which the defendant replies, "Well judge, you might as well hang me for rape too while you're at it—I got all the equipment for that too!" This joke is richer humor because the aggression is less personal and is manifested or disguised in a clever thought. The element of exhibitionism is strong here too.

One more example may illustrate the same point:

A spinster who is hungry for love has been granted one wish by a magic fairy. The woman requests that her male cat be transformed into a prince. Once the miracle is performed, the prince says to her with a quavering voice: "Now aren't you sorry you had me altered?"

The sexual joke is a special form of witticism in which the disguised aggression is a disguised sexual aggression. As an insult is not a joke, neither is an obscenity a joke. Both must disguise the aggressive component in order to become enjoyable. How this works may be illustrated with the following story:

A girl went for a hike in the Hollywood Hills and when she found a place to rest she fell asleep. When she awoke she found herself facing her favorite movie idol, who was smiling at her, and said, "I am Prince Charming and you may ask for the fulfillment of three wishes." The girl smiled back prettily and said, "I have only one wish, but that one three times."

As in any good joke, the sexual aggression in it is well disguised and hidden. It contains an aggression against the girl by suggesting that the fair sex also wants intercourse, and it is not the desire only of dirty-minded men; further, that they want it and that they are almost always ready, and that they are not quite as "virtuous" as they want the boys to believe.

A second aggressive, well disguised element in this joke is the pleasure to see the generous gentleman trapped to live up to his promise. He found his master.

Another example:

On a very hot day a woman had just put a birthday cake in the oven and decided to take a nap. Because it was so very hot she took her nap in the nude. All of a sudden she awakened and realized it was time to take the cake out of the oven. She did so, not bothering to get dressed. Holding the cake in her hands and looking for a place to put it down she heard somebody enter the service porch and quickly stepped behind the door leading to the basement. Somebody entered the kitchen, delivered something, and apparently left. She came out from behind the door and suddenly faced a man who was standing there. All that she could say was, "Oh, I thought you were the iceman."

The story employs the infantile pleasure of voyeurism by exposing and unmasking the nude woman of the story. The aggressive tendency of the joke is hidden eloquently by having the woman omit saying she thought it was the iceman who delivered the ice and then left. The implication is that, unconsciously, the woman betrayed a sexual desire and is not as innocent as a woman baking a birthday cake seems to be.

My favorite story:

A homosexual young man was standing with his friend on a street corner and leisurely watching a Brigitte Bardot type of girl wiggling by. After watching her approvingly, he turned to his friend and said, "There are moments in my life when I wish I were a lesbian."

With one swift sentence the whole world of heterosexuality was declared nonsense and an inescapable homosexual solution was offered. Again a second hostile trend is woven into the fabric of this joke—the derision of homosexuals. The offered homosexual solution of the sexual challenge is obviously acceptable only to fools.

The sexual cartoon contains the same dynamics as the obscene story or sexually-flavored joke. The illustration taken from *Esquire* magazine with the caption of "You lied" (Figure 1) is an example of extreme economy. In one sense, it vents the aggression inherent in the

"You lied!"

Figure 1

common state of disillusionment wherein the promises and great expectations of courtship never seem to be realized.

Grimm's fairy tale about the Frog King sounds so innocent but appears quite different when looked at with the jaundiced eye of the analyst:

A little girl plays with her golden ball and lets it bounce up and down. As could be expected the ball falls into the well where it cannot be reached by the now weeping princess (all of these are sexual symbols of infantile masturbation where the girl finds a way from the external genitals to the mysteries of her vagina). On the bottom of the "well" sits a frog who extracts a promise from her to marry him, like the beast in the fairy tale of Beauty and the Beast; it is hoped that the bad, dirty, beastly sex of the little frog is transformed into glorious beauty by the innocence of the virgin princess. The sexual components of the story become obvious with graphic description of the frog visiting the princess in her castle at night to cash in her promise. The frog represents a penis. Significantly, the father insists that she must keep her promise and she goes to bed with the frog. Sure enough, she learns to love her slimy bed companion, who turns out in the morning to be a lovely, beautiful, experienced prince. The girl, who is no longer innocent, has been awakened to a mature woman by the adventure of the night. In the cartoon (Figure 2) the whole story is suddenly debunked. The beast is still a beast. The story receives further cynical interpretation in the cartoon where the girl does not change ugly sex into transcendent beauty, but changes herself into a frog, meaning she has exposed undisguised "dirty" sex in herself.

The technique of the perfect sexual squelch is expressed in one very economical cartoon showing only the soles of two pair of feet in coital position and the caption: "Sam, the ceiling needs painting." Only a very

Drawing by Chas Addams; (c) 1968
The New Yorker Magazine, Inc.
Figure 2

self-assured man or very hostile one can finish what was interrupted by this remark without being driven to the point of retreat.

The most sophisticated and lovely sexual cartoon is the "Tattoed Sailor" (Figure 3). It is an excellent illustration of the fulfillment and the sublime love experience achieved through final integration of the eternal feminine by the male.

After having gained some insight into laughter, jokes, cartoons, aggression, love and sex, perhaps it can be realized that the discharge of aggression through laughter may even facilitate the free and joyful acceptance of sex. Purging the psyche with laughter may help make sexual enjoyment no longer a deadly serious duty, which one has to attend, perform correctly, and repeat at appropriate intervals. In the free expression of sexuality, responding to life freely, spontaneously, and fully, laughter will find its place and will not be felt as a disturbance or as a castration threat. As long as a man considers the sexual act as a test of strength, with the woman sitting in judgment, he may feel unfree. A man who sees sex relations less like a test, with an implied threat, and more like a welcome challenge with the implied promise of mastery and fulfillment, will enjoy it, loudly laughing when the occasion is right.

Jokes grow best on the graves of old anxieties; sexuality has been heavily loaded with anxieties for a long time. Wit gives freedom, and laughter is the expression of such freedom. Marriage and love are alive as long as the partners still know how to laugh together. The sexually experienced woman will do everything to underplay the threat of a test situation in lovemaking for the man. She will display to the man that any test is as much a challenge to her as it is to him. She will participate in the sexual experience

From: Beyond Laughter, Martin Grotjahn,
McGraw-Hill, NY., 1961
Figure 3

in a playful way until swept to the extreme of passion and love which is truly "beyond laughter."

The witty woman is feared by the insecure man because she is aggressive and therefore potentially threatening and superior. Man's potency can be witnessed—either he performs or doesn't. There is not much of a hiding place for him in bed. The woman's performance is always a secret; to guess it correctly is a motive in many jokes, such as the one of a man having intercourse with his wife who says to her, "I'm sorry dear, I didn't mean to hurt you." She replies, "You didn't hurt me. What makes you think you did?" "You moved," he answers.

Men have reason enough to fear the superiority of woman. When woman reinforces her sexual superiority by aggressive witticism, the man may react with renewed fear. The experienced man will not fear the woman after he has made certain that she wants what he has to offer. It seems as if our young people are far ahead of their parent's generation in this respect. The battle of the sexes is fought and almost settled, and has become a matter of the past generation. While we, the older generation, are still wondering whether the boys and girls nowadays try to deny sexual differences, boys seem to become more like girls and girls more like boys. They have already accepted and established a far-reaching equality between the sexes. Boys no longer wish to deny some so-called "feminine" trends in themselves and girls do not want to deny some so-called "masculine" trends in themselves, such as intelligence, courage, acceptance of sex, freedom of movement and expression, and the right to spontaneous response. In some respects equality of the sexes may be overdone but that will straighten out in time. The trends point into the future and into the right direction.

The mature man who loves a woman on an equal basis and does not insist on defensive superiority, will accept laughter with the greatest of ease. They may use it to enrich their lives—sexual and otherwise.

Bibliography

1. Freud, Sigmund: *Jokes and Their Relation to the Unconscious* (1905), Standard Edition, Vol. VIII. Hogarth Press: London, 1962.

2. Freud, Sigmund: *The Interpretation of Dreams* (1900), Standard Edition, Vols. IV and V. Hogarth Press: London:, 1962.

16/

From Humor to Happiness

Martin Grotjahn, M.D.

In the age of mastery,
man will finally be in charge of his destiny, a master
of his inner and outer reality; he will be truly an
existential man.

The human smile is the earliest sign of blissful happiness. It signifies harmony between the mother looking down at her child and the child looking up into the face of the mother. It is a unique symbol of human relation since no animal may suckle and look into the face of the mother simultaneously.

The appreciation for the comic develops when the child begins to master his motility. A clown is a man who moves in a funny way and the laughter about slapstick is based on the feeling of superiority of the child who begins to master his own movements and sees the clown either fall in that respect or employ an unusual amount of energy for a minor task. The understanding for jokes is based on a later developmental stage, namely, when the child begins to master speech and language. The first and most infantile form of joking is the pun—which is entirely based on the word. A sense of humor is an even later sign of human growth; it is generally taken as a sign of maturation. To deny a person a sense of humor is felt as a terrible indictment.

Wit gives freedom and freedom gives wit. Laughter is based on a free release of aggression in a form which is socially acceptable. Freud spent a lifetime looking for a harmless, nonaggressive joke. When he finally thought he had found one it did not stand up to later analytic scrutiny. All jokes are hidden aggressions. They must carry the aggression so well disguised and still so elegantly expressed that it does not interfere with our conscious censorship which does not tolerate open hostility, nor with our unconscious censorship which does not tolerate open hostility, nor with our unconscious awareness of the hostile trend. An undisguised expression of hostility leads to violence, not to laughter. Laughter appears where the old anxieties about aggression are sidestepped. A joke has to be told to somebody, so that his laughter confirms to the teller of the joke that the aggression is felt and recognized but is well disguised and therefore enjoyed. The psychic energy which is needed for repression is released in laughter.

Perhaps one example can illustrate the dynamics of a joke:

A married couple is enjoying a quiet evening at home when the doorbell rings. The husband opens the door and there stands a stranger who says, "I am the Boston Strangler." The husband turns around and hollers loudly to his wife, "It's for you, dear!" A very strong, hostile aggressive trend of the man against his wife is elegantly expressed in disguise so that it becomes acceptable and then is enjoyed with laughter. The release of aggression must be sudden and must occur when *the point* of the joke is understood or laughter will not occur. The moment of surprise is essential because that is the moment in which hidden aggression is suddenly allowed to be released. In the instance of the husband who turned his wife over to the Boston Strangler, it is a sudden understanding of the man's stepping aside, leaving it to his wife to meet her probably well-deserved fate in the hands of the Strangler.

Aggression may also be expressed in the form of total absurdity. Many stories about a psychiatrist follow this pattern, as for instance in the story of the psychiatrist who greets a new patient in consultation. The patient enters the doctor's office with a little bird perched on his head. The psychiatrist looks at the strange scene and asks his usual opening question, "What can I do for you?" Whereupon, the bird answers, "Get this man off my ass." The absurdity is again a disguised attack on all psychiatrists; they live in another world, in a world of craziness.

The enjoyment of jokes is based on a liberation of aggression and therefore is related to sadism and to ambivalence. The wit as a character and as a person has not yet overcome the problems of his ambivalence. He lives—and laughs—in the borderline field between love and hate. The wit is not a dangerous man, as every woman knows, because he is not loving enough to make love, not aggressive enough to rape. He sits back and laughs.

Humor is not sadistic and humor is not an expression of a regressed, repressed, or disguised aggression. Therefore, humor does not lead to loud laughter but to a silent smile. Humor is related to masochism or to the quiet acceptance of suffering. It does not imply freedom to express aggression but it implies silent resignation and a sad acceptance of life as it is lived with death as its final solution.

There is the special place of the Jewish Joke, of which Freud was so fond. Most of his examples presented and analyzed in his famous book of jokes are taken from Jewish folklore. The truly Jewish Jokes are rather sad and when they are well told by our Jewish friends they are enjoyed with deep satisfaction. No other people have made themselves so mercilessly and so consistently the butt of their own joke and no other people do that so well and in such a penetrating way. In its pitiless aggression, the Jewish Joke is related to sadistic witticism. In its sadness and melancholic flavor, the Jewish Joke carries a masochistic meaning of true humor. It is as if a Jewish man tells his enemies: Do you know us well enough to hate us? We know ourselves better and we can give much better examples of what should be hated in us. We know ourselves well and we can give the best examples of our short-comings. But, then comes the great reassuring message of the Jewish Joke. It is as if the Jewish man tells himself, his friends, and his enemies, "This is the way we are, the way we always have been, and the way we always will be!"

For the enjoyment of jokes three people are needed for laughter. One person conceives the joke, which is directed against a second person. It must be told to a third person so that the laughter shows his under-standing for the hidden aggression and approval of the dis-guise. In humor, only one person is needed: The humorist smiles at himself and at human tragedy with resigned and forgiving attitude toward himself. He accepts his weakness as essentially human. He has overcome aggression, hostility, and ambivalence. His acceptance is a sign of his maturity. In humor we see the symbolic reestablishment of the happy union between mother and baby. In humor we repeat and reexperi-ence the first smile of blissful infancy. The man accepts the boy in himself finally. Humor in women is of slightly different, symbolic meaning; it is an acceptance and love of the mother and of her troubled baby in herself.

Freud had a tragic outlook on reality, which amounted practically to an appeal for endurance. Freud was fond of quoting Lichtenstein and said it is best not to be born at all—but this happens only to a very few. Another time in his free style of writing which he reserved for letters to friends, Freud compared life to a baby shirt: too short and full of shit.

Freud once defined happiness as the final fulfillment of an old and repressed childhood desire. Happiness is self when the infant's blissful existence, the harmony of the infant with his mother, is reexperienced, either in reality of in symbolic representation. Such rediscovery of an old and long repressed childhood situation must not take place in a regressive way, as in schizophrenia, but in a creative way. In such an existential experience of happiness a person finally feels himself the master of his destiny. He feels himself the master of his inner and outer environment. He repeats in a mature and realistic way what he felt once in the child's magic-mystic omnipotence of infantile narcissism.

We are entering an age in which realistic mastery will become possible. It even will become more democratic and will not remain a privilege of the outstanding few and of the "beautiful people." Mastery is moving into the reach of everybody who strives for it. The coming age will be an age of mastery. We will manage to master reality and man will no longer need to adjust to his environment; man can now create or adjust the world to his needs. The burden of adjustment has shifted from man to his environment. This is what our young people try to tell us with their protest. They tell us loudly, "The world and we are different—the world must change." Soon they will have the power and energy to do so.

177

True humor originates in the kind acceptance of the infant by the mother, even if the child is naughty, greedy, or dirty. True humor is the acceptance of the man by himself, of his unconscious, of his limitations, and of the unfinished search for truth. The mother finally accepts her imperfect son in resigned love. By then, this process is no longer reenacted in reality but is symbolized and experienced in symbol. Or it is introjected and takes place within the person and no longer outside of him. The acceptance then becomes a harmony between conscious and unconscious, superego and id, introjected mother image and residual trends from the past.

Jesus knew what it meant to accept one's self; but he did not ask us to love our neighbor more than ourselves. Loving him just as much as ourselves was good enough and would do. Wisdom asks more than self-acceptance; it asks for acceptance of death as the unavoidable end of human existence.

In the coming age of mastery mankind will learn to master the pain of dying but death will be with us as long as man lives. Therefore, the final acceptance of death will always be waiting for man on the way from maturity to wisdom. In the age of mastery, man will finally be in charge of his destiny, a master of his inner and outer reality; he will be truly an existential man.

Freud thought that happiness is experienced when an old childhood wish is fulfilled—in the last analysis when the blissful union between the loving mother and her baby is reestablished. It is this situation which is so essentially human and which is also the situation where the first human smile occurs.

This union can be achieved symbolically in the experience of beauty, or peace, or truth. It also is expressed in deepening feeling for one's self, an experience of one's own identity: when you are happy, you know who you are. In a sad way this union with the symbol of the mother can be experienced in the final union with death.

The human symbiosis between mother and child, like the human symbiosis between two friends or between two people in love, is the essence of happiness. To live in such love and live together in trust and in beauty is to "live with God."

17/

The New Laughter

Werner M. Mendel, M.D.

A walk with Martin Grot-jahn sparkles with life.

Today for the first time in the history of man, we in the United States face the realistic possibility of a life of relative leisure, comfort, and creative opportunity. In previous times only a few aristocrats found themselves in the difficult position of facing such a life. To live such leisure creatively with satisfaction and joy is more difficult than to live a life of work and toil. An unsuccessful life of leisure will seem like a sentence in which the person is condemned to "having nothing to do," to filling time, to merely living a life waiting to die.

We are not prepared for the life which our technology has created for us. The value system of our culture, which is reflected in our child-rearing practices and in our school system, was appropriate for the pioneering, agrarian society of two hundred years ago. It has little relevance to the realities of 1970. Many of society's problems today can be attributed to the difficulties caused by the transition period between deprivation and plenty, between toil and leisure, between drudgery and a life of creativity. Our national attitudes about work, thrift, productivity, and recreation are out of touch with our reality.

The fruits of the technological society which our generation has helped to create is most clearly noted in the shrinking workweek. In two generations the workweek has decreased from sixty to thirty-five hours per week. We are left with time which we are generally unprepared to use for our growth and pleasure. The increased leisure time for many unprepared Americans has become a period of frantic activity, a time to be filled. These unhappy people can be seen living their leisure time by rushing each long weekend in their camper on a bumper to bumper freeway, the motorcycle tied to the front and the motorboat on a trailer hitched to the rear, the barbecue and the portable color TV mounted on top while inside there is a supply of Scotch or pot to help endure the leisure moments. Within the next fifteen years the four day and three day workweek will become a fact of life. How will people use or endure this leisure? What can we do to help our children prepare for this leisure time?

The American public school system, which is based on the puritan, agricultural, work-oriented ethic, is essentially anti-pleasure, anti-creativity, anti-joy, and anti-leisure, and anti-laughter. If it is left unaltered we will insure that the next generation will face the new world of leisure with guilt, with boredom, without creativity, and without the laughter of freedom. We are now laying the groundwork for the alienation, the depression, and the impaired self-esteem of our children in a world of relative leisure.

Our child-rearing practices and educational programs must prepare the children who are to exist in the world of tomorrow to live a rich, creative life in a world which offers leisure. Just as our grandparents prepared us to live in a world of work, competition, upward striving, and drudgery, we must help our children to remember that play and jokes and fun are significant and worthwhile aspects of life. We must not train them to forget that life can be lived lightheartedly and creatively. We must instill a new system of values which is based on the realities of the 1970s.

Formerly, in the process of socializing the young human being we introduced him to the "seriousness of life" and demanded that he give up his joyful play and his selective inattention to reality. We demanded of the small child that he give up his creative manipulation of reality in favor of learning skills which would help him to get ahead in the upward striving society. Now we must teach our children to continue the laughter based on the joy of recognizing new and idiosyncratic interpretations of reality. Seeing new relationships produces the laughter of creativity which is closely allied to art but which is not at all related to the workaday world. Normally, and without the interference of the adult world, the child knows how to play and how to enjoy leisure. He knows the joke of playful reinterpretation of reality and he enjoys the laughter accompanying it. We must become more sophisticated in our approach to happiness. For too long we have conceptualized happiness simply as the absence of drudgery and unhappiness. Now we can begin to recognize that to be happy one must be appropriately trained. We can encourage behavior in our child-rearing and educational procedures which prepare for enjoyment of freedom and leisure just as formerly we needed to develop techniques for tolerating the workaday world of coping, of drivenness, and of drudgery. We need to make schools truly places where our children obtain the tools with which to learn, to create for pleasure, to recreate enjoyment in the artistic works of others. We need to instill the attitudes which allow the study of literature to be a joyous experience in and of itself without necessarily preparing the student to be a teacher of literature who will work at literature. We need to provide experiences for children which help them to learn that to create produces freedom and happiness. Creativity does not need to be for the marketplace and it does not need to be rewarded with material symbols of success.

It is quite evident that our public school curricula and teaching practices are far removed from these goals of preparing students for the world of leisure. Only when our child-rearing practices and our public school educational systems have been changed, can the universities respond similarly. Only then can they return to the function of the university as a community of scholars who, without drivenness and with joy, join together in obtaining and using the tools of the culture for the pleasure of knowledge. Only when the universities have a curriculum which prepares the student for life rather than for a job, which prepares him for happiness rather than for a salary, which gives him the tools for tapping the collective resources of the culture rather than for the exploitation of technology for the production of marketable services and goods, will we have an educational system which reflects the reality created by our technology. If we are to change from merely enduring leisure to enjoying leisure and living leisure, we must rely on the development of techniques in each of our lives for having fun and for being creative in our existence.

The word creativity here is not meant in the usual sense of painting, or playing music, or writing books. I mean creativity in the sense of playful giving up of consensually validated reality for the purpose of seeing new relationships and new sequences in juxtaposition. Creativity in this sense is closely related to the lighthearted playful recreation of reality found in fun, in some jokes, in humor, and in happiness.

The young child laughs when he can make meaning of the meaningless world around him. He laughs when he has mastery over his own anxiety in games and stories. As he becomes older he laughs when he is relieved of pain or he laughs when someone is the victim of his angry thoughts. He learns to smile, to hide his hostility and he laughs at himself to reduce the pain of the injured self-esteem. Such laughter and such humor which derive from a world of work, of guilt, and of drivenness will not sustain us when we are "damned" to an existence of leisure. Martin Grotjahn said that in the future the man to be envied will not be the one who has power or who has wealth or who is successful. Rather it will be the one who has a meaningful existence, who can assign meaning to his work or to his job. I am somewhat more optimistic than Dr. Grotjahn. I think we can predict our world clearly enough to prepare our children for it. We can give them the tools to learn to laugh lightheartedly and with leisure. Really, all we have to do is to stop interfering with a normal process found in the child. We must stop extinguishing the joy of creativity found in the young child. He already knows the happiness of selective inattention to reality. He is already prepared to be happy in the experience of enjoying the passage of time. It is our child-rearing practices which transmit the system of values which extinguishes the playful joyousness of the young child. Later on he needs alcohol or drugs to reinstate such a laughter, such playful joy in altering reality. Perhaps a look at the type of humor is a better clue to the differences between the new and the old generation. We of the adult world laugh to express hostility, to hurt ourselves, to relieve tension or to cover guilt. Small children laugh in the playful *recreation* of reality. Some of the young people who are serious critics of our society have maintained the ability to enjoy playful laughter in spite of society's attempts at educating and socializing the fun out of them. They still refuse to laugh with anger, with guilt, or with hurt.

185

In the future the man to be envied is the one who has the tools with which to enjoy a light-hearted existence of a creatively-lived leisure time. Our grandparents had pleasure from working hard to create the technology which makes possible human existence of relative leisure. We are heirs to this technology. Our children are the heirs of the leisure created by this technology. For the first time since the expulsion of Adam and Eve we have the opportunity to return to the Garden of Eden.

Man ate of the tree of knowledge and developed his world of technology. This technology has now made it possible for us to return to the Garden of Eden where we can eat of the tree of life whose fruits are conflict-free laughter, nonmarketable creativity, and noncompetitive happiness.

Contributors

RICHARD BELLMAN, Ph.D., Professor of Mathematics, Electrical Engineering and Medicine, University of Southern California, Los Angeles

JOSEPH BOSKIN, Ph.D., Professor of History and Afro-American Studies, Acting Director, American Studies Program, Boston University

ART BUCHWALD, Political Columnist

MARTIN GROTJAHN, M.D., Clinical Professor of Psychiatry, University of Southern California School of Medicine; Supervising and Training Analyst of the Southern California Psychoanalytic Institute, Los Angeles

MICHAEL GROTJAHN, M.D., Psychiatrist, San Francisco

LAWRENCE S. KUBIE, M.D., D.Sc., Senior Associate in Research and Training, The Sheppard and Enoch Pratt Hospital, Towson, Maryland; Clinical Professor of Psychiatry, University of Maryland School of Medicine, Baltimore

ROBERT LITMAN, M.D., Professor of Psychiatry, University of Southern California School of Medicine; Co-Director and Chief Psychiatrist of the Suicide Prevention Center, Los Angeles; Supervising and Training Analyst of the Southern California Psychoanalytic Institute, Los Angeles

LORI MENDEL, President, Mara Books, Inc., Los Angeles

WERNER MENDEL, M.D., Professor of Psychiatry, University of Southern California School of Medicine, Los Angeles

Contributors

ALEXANDER S. ROGAWSKI, M.D., Clinical Professor of Psychiatry and Director, Division of Social and Community Psychiatry, University of Southern California School of Medicine, Los Angeles; Supervising and Training Analyst of the Southern California Psychoanalytic Institute, Los Angeles

ROBERT SKLAR, Ph.D., Associate Professor of History, University of Michigan, Ann Arbor

EDWARD STAINBROOK, Ph.D., M.D., Professor and Chairman, Department of Human Behavior, University of Southern California School of Medicine, Los Angeles

LILLA VESZY-WAGNER, Ph.D., Member of the British Psychoanalytical Society, London

CARLO WEBER, Ph.D., Jesuit Priest, psychologist; formerly an Assistant Professor of Psychology and Director of Psychological Services at Loyola University, Los Angeles; Chief of the Division of Training and Consultation with the Los Angeles County Department of Mental Health.

Credits

Dr. Grotjahn's chapter, "Jewish Jokes and the Relationship to Masochism," is reprinted with the permission of the Hillside Hospital in Glen Oaks, New York and the International Universities Press, Inc. This article first appeared in the *Journal of the Hillside Hospital,* Volume X, Numbers 3 and 4, 1961. "Laughter and Sex" is reprinted with the permission of the journal, *Medical Aspects of Human Sexuality,* September, 1969, pp. 92–96. "Laughter in Psychotherapy" is reprinted by permission from VOICES, the Art and Science of Psychotherapy, Vol. 5, No. 2, 1969. By permission of McGraw-Hill Book Company, Blakiston Division, the Figure 3 cartoon which appeared in Dr. Grotjahn's book, *Beyond Laughter,* page 116, published by McGraw-Hill Book Company in 1957. Figure 1 cartoon is reproduced by permission of Esquire Magazine, 1960; and Figure 2 cartoon by Chas Addams, 1968, is reproduced by permission of the New Yorker Magazine, Inc. The picture of Martin Grotjahn, M.D., is being reproduced with the permission of the *Medical Tribune* and the Black Star Photo Agency in New York. "It Isn't Just MIRV," copyright by Art Buchwald.

 **mara
BOOKS**

Creative Art By
dot Design, San Francisco, California
Photon Typography in Optima and Book Manufacture By
Edwards Brothers, Inc., Ann Arbor, Michigan